HEADS *or* TALES

HEADS *or* TALES

RECOLLECTIONS OF A SOUTHERN FAMILY

Ann Rowland Hamlin

XULON PRESS

Xulon Press
2301 Lucien Way #415
Maitland, FL 32751
407.339.4217
www.xulonpress.com

Unless otherwise indicated, Scripture quotations taken from the King James Version (KJV) – *public domain*.

Printed in the United States of America

Paperback ISBN-13: 978-1-6322-1996-1
Ebook ISBN-13: 978-1-6322-1997-8

DEDICATION

THIS BOOK IS dedicated to John Head, Charles Head and Doris Riggins. Without their contributions, this book would not be possible. Thank you for the memories, stories, photographs, and time shared.

This book is written in honor of my grandparents, John Arthur and Kansie Whitmire Head. Their life, journey and love have no expiration date.

This book is also written in honor of my parents, Harold M. and Annie Head Rowland. They were two of the best people and greatest parents in the world.

And finally, this book is written in honor of my husband, Clinton Eugene Hamlin, who left this world way too soon, but taught me so much while here on earth. He loved this little girl from Central and literally gave me the world.

ACKNOWLEDGEMENTS

I WOULD LIKE TO thank my cousin Joanne Hawkins Carter for organizing visits and interactions to make these stories come to life. I am also grateful for her help in reviewing the book.

I would also like to thank my cousins Hellen Hawkins Reeves, Margaret Hawkins, and Barbara Hawkins McMahon for sharing information in the meetings. Thanks also to Hellen for sharing some of her family research.

I would also like to thank my brothers David, John, Cecil and Tom Rowland for information they remembered and shared. More importantly, thank you for letting me be your little sister all of these years.

TABLE OF CONTENTS

INTRODUCTION

FROM TIME TO time as I see a rocking chair on a porch, or feel the warmth of the sun shining down on me after a rain, or experience other remembrances from my past, my mind goes back in time. It goes to home and to a more simple life. It goes to a time and place that no longer exists. My childhood flashes before me. I blink my eyes and I find myself here. As I reminisce about people and places, my reflections leave me asking the same question. How did I get here, today, in the present time? This question recounts a few steps that I may have remembered at the time; a recall of decisions made and actions taken that led to certain relationships, careers and places. As I try to bring my past to the present, the reflection on that question leads me to some phenomenal people. Those reflections lead me down the roads of actions taken and lives that lived on a grand scale. The lives of many that came together, made their journeys, faced their challenges and fears, and paved the road for me to be here today. After the loss of my parents, part of the grieving process for me was to learn more about them. Those reflections have become more frequent over the past few years. The reflections leave more questions than answers; ones needed for closure and moving forward. As I learned more about my family, I became grateful and thankful that I am not the one in control. I am thankful that the author and finisher of my life story is One so much greater than I. One who could take challenges, obstacles, failure and success and make beauty out of it all.

As we make our friends, but are born into family, it is those family relationships, both present and past, which have guided me. The origin of my name, my DNA, and inherited traits and characteristics that made me my own person and guided my likes and dislikes, are just some of the benefits of looking back. Reflections have brought emotional and spiritual well-being. As with most everything, we need to look beyond the obvious to find the truth and the true meaning of life. Whether there is success or failure, there are lessons to be learned in order to find a deeper meaning for our purpose. Looking back over generations has helped me to see a much larger picture in place, one in which I was guided, but, nevertheless, now still have some control in how the story ends.

As I began my reflections upon family more intently after the loss of my mother, some memories told a few stories and answered some questions. Before my dad passed away, he shared stories that none of his kids or grand kids had heard before. With my mom passing away just months before, his stories were necessary and therapeutic for him. Little did I realize until later what a treasure he had given us. Even with his stories, there were so many blanks to fill. Lots of unanswered questions that I had never bothered to ask popped so quickly into my mind.

Stories from my aunt and uncles have filled in some of the blanks. My mom's sister, Doris and her two brothers, John and Charles, shared numerous stories about their lives and growing up. My brothers and cousins were able to fill in some of the blanks as well. As I heard the stories, I began to appreciate my history even more. As they shared information, I learned so many things not found in history books. Dates and names may be found in those books, but the information and storytelling made me want to search for more. Learning more incredible stories and facts prompted in me the desire to share with others and especially the younger generations of my nieces and nephews and their children and grandchildren. It is my belief that we are given stories, opportunities or experiences in order to share. With the rampant availability of technology to do everything for us today, without any reflection of how it was done prior to that technology, these stories were waiting to be told. Another reason for sharing is centered on the fact that as times do change, which is inevitable, there are some things that remain constant and never go out of style. Integrity and faith are values that can guide us. If we live our lives by what we believe in, rather than in what is happening around us, those values can lead us to answers and guide us on our journey to remarkable destinations.

We are often taught lessons so we can teach others. This look into my family was so much more than genealogy. While genealogy certainly helped to fill in some of the blanks from generations before, it only set the stage for the personalities and characters we will meet in this story. Having much respect for the heritage of my maternal grandparents, the story is about them. It is about their children. It is filled with tales and memories of growing up and living in the South. It is filled with lessons they learned along the way and ones we are still living today.

As I am the narrator of this story about my grandparents, they will be affectionately referred to as Granny and /or Grandpa in the stories throughout the book as I try to chronicle their spirit. Through this journey into the lives of the Head family, it is hoped to capture and preserve momentary glimpses of family history and memories for future generations. Through personal stories, there are tidbits of American history, as chronicled by recollections of tales passed down or remembrances of those who lived through some of these times. As the personal stories themselves may not have much appeal to some, it is hoped that the information and facts generated from thought and research will reflect the culture of early Americana in the South. Even better, it is hoped to challenge the reader to ask questions to those still living today in their family in order to reflect upon their own history, generate their own memories, or possibly receive healing in an unexpected way. Tell your stories and let your history live on in others through traditions and story. Memories, even faded ones, have value.

The main characters in this story were born six months apart in 1897, roughly forty miles from each other, and separated by a state line. John Arthur Head was born in South Carolina, and Kansie Edna Whitmire was born in North Carolina. Twenty-five years later their worlds became one as they were married. They eventually became prominent citizens of Central, South Carolina, owning several businesses and many acres of land. More importantly, they also became parents to nine children, grandparents to 25 grandchildren, and great grandparents to numerous great grandchildren. Thus, their descendants were truly Carolinians. Their work ethic and character reflected their family's identity for generations to come. Characteristics of courage, strength, intelligence, discipline, love and a strong faith in God came to mind as I learned about their beginnings and making their way. One can imagine with a family this large, there are many tales to be told and remembered in writing for sharing with generations to come. It is said that by writing things down, it is possible to create a picture of a person, an action, a place or a time. With that intent, it is hoped the stories shared will demonstrate those characteristics and many more.

My grandparents' lives not only impacted their children, but the numerous people they encountered in the upstate of South Carolina and western North Carolina over a life time. From struggles for survival to hard work and ingenuity, they reared a family, created a home and influenced a town and provided hope for many people. Their challenges and struggles were not unique to them. Glimpses of their stories may be reflected in either memories or in some of the stories that you may have heard about your family members and others while growing up "back in the day."

My grandparents established landmarks, both physical and spiritual, for their children and the generations that follow. Landmarks help to identify both properties and paths to take. They serve as points of interest. They can guide the weary traveler to a place of peace and comfort. For others they may validate information already known or help them to reach what they are searching for. Landmarks are valuable and important. They help to serve as a guide and can help to avoid danger or getting lost. They help to map out destiny. Landmarks are often thought of in the form of mountains, rivers, buildings, signs or land. For this purpose of telling my grandparents' story, their landmarks serve in the way of stories, memories, pictures, small mementos, names and land. They serve as a strong heritage and reminder of what can be done moving forward. "Remove not the ancient landmark, which thy fathers have set." (Proverbs 22:28, King James Version).

For those of you still fortunate to have family accessible, visit with them. Give of your time. Talk to them and ask questions and find out information about their past, your past. Learn information about your heritage. What stories can they tell? Age may have slowed their steps a bit, greyed their hair and weakened their body and mind, but I bet their spirit, enthusiasm and ability to recall some stories remain strong. Too often we see that memories die with their owner because time takes us unaware and it runs out. If you are not fortunate enough to have your family available or even have fond memories for that matter, then be the positive source for others. Create landmarks that others would want to search for. Establish landmarks that others would not only want to find, but also follow, hold on to, and share with others.

Chapter One

EARLY YEARS

IT IS SAID that a picture is worth a thousand words, but I contend that a thousand words and more paint a beautiful picture. The words shared represent brushstrokes that came together and made colorful stories and served as the canvas for a masterpiece painting. The background in the painting takes you back in time and through the years with some of the paint dried and left with cracks or stains. The foreground of the painting reflects present day, with portions remaining vibrant and priceless.

In order for the most accurate portrait of my grandparents and their children to be made, the era in which they lived, what their everyday life was like, and the obstacles faced need to be discussed. These conditions seem unbelievable and unimaginable to many, but the knowledge of these conditions as told by family members, help attest to the will and strength of both my grandparents and my parents' generations. These descriptions set the stage for many of the stories told. Most of the conditions and landscape of the time are vivid and revealed within those stories. Through this picture, there will be a glimpse of living in the early to mid-1900's in western North Carolina and upstate South Carolina, where landmarks were in need of development.

In the early 1900's, the majority of the South was rural or farm land. There was limited or no access to electricity, indoor plumbing or refrigeration until after World War II. The basic luxuries taken for granted today were nonexistent. The lack of telephones, television, and availability of only radios limited communication and isolated people. Much of the isolation was also due to lack of cars and paved roads. Travel was by foot, horseback, mule or wagon. Most people walked everywhere they went. Long distance travel needed to be planned. Wagons could travel roughly around 8 to 20 miles per day depending on the weather and road conditions, while travel by train became an option for some as the railroad system was largely built by the 1900's, making train travel possible for people as well as for shipping cargo[1]

Even though the Ford Motor Company was around in the early 1900's, it would take years before cars would be available and affordable. In 1927, the Ford Model A car was the company's second market success after the mass-produced Model T succeeded for close to 20 years.[2] In addition to lack of affordability for most, outside of large cities, there weren't many roads accessible and drivable.

Counties in the upstate of South Carolina and western North Carolina were sparsely settled. One could go miles before passing a house. Roads often were nothing more than trails going over hills. Main industry was farming and the main product was corn which could be sold. Most all supplies were raised at home and very few articles bought in stores, the nearest of which could be miles away.

Farming was the main way of life. Most everything was done by hand. Horses, mules and people provided most of the power behind the farming. The animals were affordable, dependable, and could handle various terrains better than machinery. Any equipment or machinery that was available was simple and very limited. Farmers were self-sufficient either by growing or trading for most everything they needed. Living off the land was vital to many. Very little cash was in circulation. Most farmers operated on credit from merchants and paid the debt off at harvest times. Hunting and fishing helped to supplement food for some tables and offered a chance to get away from the drudgery of everyday work, with only a little down time for sport and enjoyment. Days were long and hard with work from before sunrise to long after sunset on the farm and in the home as well. Steady and endless work was necessary to sustain the farm and home.

Cooking was almost constant and usually centered on a wood-stove and cast iron cookware. Food preparation often began before sunrise. Fire needed to be stoked. Cows had to be milked. Eggs gathered and so on. Milk that was not used in the daily cooking or drinking was left to clabber so that butter could be made. Cooking lasted throughout the day as meats and whatever vegetables were available had to be cooked and three meals served if you were lucky. Meats were cured to help them last as long as possible with no refrigeration available. Vegetables and fruits were dried, canned, or fresh when available depending on the season. Sundays were usually special because big meals would be cooked and served, especially if company was invited to dine after church. The vast amount of cooking that needed to be done, especially in large families, did lend itself to the teaching of younger ones to cook. Everyone had to pitch in. Teaching and sharing of recipes for cooking and preserving were passed down from generation to generation.

Cleaning the home, scrubbing and sweeping floors, laundry and such activities were often daily chores in addition to cooking. Sewing talents were also passed from generation to generation. From making clothes and mending tears to embroidery, knitting and crochet, these talents were taught and passed on. The isolation and necessity for hard work for survival definitely led to the ability to take care of family and forced a sense of independence. Children of all ages were given chores to perform which were necessary for survival, but helped to develop a work ethic, as well.

In addition to farming and growing corn, growing cotton became an important business as well in the South. The industrial revolution brought cotton mills to the Carolinas and gave them another option for their livelihood. The majority of rivers or ponds with running water seemed to sprout cotton mills, along with hope for those who migrated from farms to new industry within the region. [3]

Small country churches were around, or cottage prayer meetings were held from home to home. Schools were not in abundance. Education was limited, and the school year often was influenced by farming and harvest times. Some teens did not attend school and worked in fields or factories. There were very few books and supplies for school. In the early years, all grades were held in the same building. For any spare time for kids, toys were fairly simple or homemade. Marbles, checkers, slingshots, yo-yos, and a few bicycles were around.

Along with all of the everyday obstacles to confront and overcome, my grandparents' generation lived through World War I and The Great Depression, and World War II, which my parents' generation remembered, as well. Despite the struggles, they overcame, they survived, they taught and they developed strong generations that followed in their footsteps. These generations developed physical landmarks that remain standing today. They developed spiritual ones, as well, that have been passed down and remain intact and practiced.

Chapter Two

A TALE OF TWO CAROLINAS

To know my grandparents, the land they grew up on and labored on was vital not only to their beginnings, but instrumental in developing their character and personalities. Locations shaped their struggles, livelihood, enjoyment, determination and destination. Legends, geography and landscapes influenced their personalities and developed the foundation for landmarks by carving struggle and uncertainty while others revealed beauty and wonder.

Rosman, North Carolina, is located in Transylvania County. It has the distinction of being known previously by many different names. "The post office mailing address for the town was Calvert in 1888 and changed to Jeptha in 1890. The heart of Rosman was established when folks arrived by train and were welcomed to Toxaway at the train depot. The post office was changed in early 1900 to the name of Toxaway to match the name of the depot. Near the town was an ancient Indian trading path leading to South Carolina known as Eastatoe Path or Trail that had been traveled for hundreds of years by the Cherokees. The path crossed the French Broad River in the Rosman area. Trappers and traders knew the area as Eastatoe Ford. Because of confusion with a resort town of Lake Toxaway located some 10 miles away and the local townspeople referring to their community as Eastatoe, the name was changed to Eastatoe in 1903." [4] "In 1905, a local industrialist, Joseph Silversteen, gave the town the new name of Rosman, coming from two of his business associates, Joseph Rosenthal and Morris Osmansky. Rosman prospered and became Transylvania County's commercial center with thriving leather and lumber industries. Silversteen was a tanner by trade and in 1902 developed the Toxaway Tanning Company and several other companies in the area. In 1910 he established the Gloucester Lumber Company. He purchased over 20,000 acres of land from George Vanderbilt for the lumber. Trains hauled in logs from a logging railroad and camps reaching into what today is the Pisgah National Forest area. In addition to the local businesses, the opening of The Gloucester General Store (also known as The Company Store) served as a community hub and business center for Rosman. Built in 1910 by Joseph Silversteen, it was in business for over 70 years and became the spot for buying staples and socializing as well. Employees from Silversteen's plants and mills were paid in coupons that could be exchanged for goods at the store. The store stayed open late each night until the last logging train had run and supplies for the loggers in camp could be purchased."[5]

Rosman sits on the eastern boundary of Pisgah National Forest and the French Broad River runs through it. The French Broad is thought to be the third-oldest river in the world. It begins around Rosman and flows into Tennessee. It is locally referred to as North Fork, West Fork, East Fork and Middle Fork. Bent Creek, Mills River, and Davidson River are its three major streams and tributaries. In an article from *Southern Living*, the French Broad is discussed as follows: "A mountain river is the path of least resistance revealed by water, and the French Broad's curvature historically dictated the placement of villages, towns, and industry. It is traced by drover trails from the 1700s, which evolved into a historic route known as the Buncombe Turnpike. The river once transported explorers, livestock, and lumber through areas that were otherwise hard to reach... Like every waterway, this river is constantly in flux—because of weather, time, and human hands—but its ability to evoke awe is enduring." [6]

Transylvania County was founded in 1861 with its name derived from the Transylvania Colony : *trans* "across" and *silva* "woods". "With mountains rising over 6,000 feet, forests stretching from end to end, deep gorges weaved with streams and geological marvels emerging from ancient volcanoes, the county offers nature on a grand scale. There are over 250 waterfalls in the county, the highest concentration in North America. The Blue Ridge Parkway forges through parts of the county, and has views of the Appalachian Mountains. The highest point, Chestnut Knob, 6,025 feet, lies northwest of the county seat Brevard. The cradle of forestry became the birthplace of America's modern forestry movement." [7]

A chain of waterfalls along the North and South Carolina border is the highest series of falls in eastern North America, plummeting hundreds of feet. "The upper falls are in North Carolina and falls 411 feet while the lower falls in South Carolina drop 400 feet and are on the Whitewater River, which spills into Lake Jocassee. The falls get their name from the foamy white water that forms as it cascades over the rocks and terrain and falls into the river below. There are over twenty-five waterfalls in Oconee County, South Carolina, the most prominent being the Lower Whitewater Falls. The name Oconee derives from the Cherokees and has several interpretations, one of the most popular being 'water eyes of the hills,' in reference to the area's many waterfalls and streams".[8]

Salem is located in Oconee County, South Carolina. It was established in 1907 and was "centered hub-like in a wheel formation of foothill communities that included Burnt Tanyard, Cheohee, Danville, Fall Creek, Flat Shoals, Jocasse, Little River, Smeltzer, Stamp Creek, Talley, Tamassee and Whitewater.[9] The town today lies in a hilly area in close proximity to Lake Keowee, Keowee-Toxaway State Park, Lake Jocassee and Devils Fork State Park. The North Carolina-South Carolina border passes several miles north of Salem. Oconee County is the only county in South Carolina bordering on two states—Georgia and North Carolina. Located in the northwest corner of South Carolina at the foot of the Blue Ridge Mountains, the region was home to Cherokee Indians until the Revolutionary War, when they were driven from all except the northernmost section. "Famous Cherokee landmarks of Keowee Indian town and Fort Prince George site are in the Salem area under the waters of Lake Keowee. Oconee County was created in 1868, from the western half of Pickens County. After the Civil war, districts were changed to counties, and Pickens district was divided into what are now Pickens and Oconee Counties with the Keowee River serving as the dividing line."[10]

In the 1960's Duke Power Company began a power-generating project that resulted in the creation of Lake Jocassee in 1973, just above Lake Keowee." The two lakes were developed as a part of the Keowee-Toxaway complex. Included in the complex is the Oconee Nuclear Station along with the Keowee, Jocassee, and Bad Creek hydroelectric stations. [11] "The Atlanta and Richmond Airline Railroad (later part of the Southern Railway) arrived in Oconee in the 1870's. The town of Seneca, chartered in 1874, was built at the spot where the northern and southern section of the road was joined. The town of Westminster was also established on the railroad in 1874. Industrial development followed these transportation improvements. Oconee joined many Piedmont counties in becoming home to a number of textile mills. In 1893 the mill village of Newry was established." [12]

The upstate of South Carolina has an intriguing history. Native Americans and wild beasts lived simultaneously in a territory full of green forests, clear streams and Blue Ridge Mountains rising in the foreground. The Cherokees claimed it for their favorite hunting ground and established Indian villages while the lower territories were developed by white men. Many stories account for the history of the names in the area and offer differing tales as legends often do. A synopsis of the recount from author and historian E. Don Herd, Jr., attests to one of the most famous legends.

> The Indian town was called Keowee, place of the Mulberry. Tradition has it that Isaqueena, Indian maiden daughter of a chief of one of the Choctow Indian tribes, was kidnapped and held captive by a Cherokee chief. Her name was Cateechee in Cherokee. Both names meant deer's head. As she lived in Cherokee

nation, a white man, James Francis and his two sons Allen and Henry traded with the Cherokees. An initial attraction between the Indian maiden and Allen Francis blossomed into love. One evening as she moved among war council members of the tribe refilling their war pipes, she overheard of their plot to attack and wipe out the trading post where her love lived. Knowing she had to alert the fort, she escaped from Keowee in the upstate and went to Ninety-Six in the mid-lands by horse to warn that the Cherokees were planning an attack. On her expedition that night and all of the next day, she crossed rivers, climbed hills, traversed woods and crossed fields. She measured her progress by naming the creeks and rivers she crossed. There was Six Mile Creek, Twelve Mile River, Eighteen Mile Creek, Three and Twenty and Six and Twenty Creeks. As she reached her destination, she reckoned she had traveled ninety-six miles to reach the fort. These landmarks were named to honor her heroic ride and remain today along with a mill community in Pickens County, businesses, women's clubs, historical organizations and societies by using either of her names. Other names originated from this legend as well according to Don Herd. After this event happened, Cateechee was later captured along with Allen Francis and returned to Indian Country. Their lives were spared and they both lived in the Indian village for a couple of years as they planned their escape. One day after getting caught in a storm, Cateechee failed to return to the village. Allen went to find her and they hid for a time in the forest in a big hollow tree. As the search for them ensued, one Indian chief came across the hollowed shelter and called it a stump house and the name for Stump House Mountain was born. The couple was not found in the shelter as Allen was in the woods making a canoe. Cateechee was on the banks of the river as they approached. When she saw them, she remembered seeing a duck dive into the falls and she dove into the falls just as the duck had done. She landed on a ledge behind the falls where the duck had a nest. Believing her to have been killed, the Indians left. Allen came to her rescue and they later left by canoe and floated down the river. At some point, they left the river and were able to travel and reach family. The plunging of the Indian maiden into the falls gave it the name Isaqueena Falls.[13]

The historical colonial site of Ninety-Six gives us a window into the past of the Carolinas according to authors Dunkerly and Williams. "This little-known town was the center of activity for the region in its day ...and the Ninety-Six story touches on many important themes of colonial history, including exploration and settlement, Native American relations, the growth of early American society, African American history, the French and Indian War, the American Revolution and many other topics. Hunters roamed the area and evolved into more complex groups. Cherokee was the dominant Native American presence and would draw trade from the coast, which lead to the building of the town, due to the importance of its roads. Located along the Cherokee Path, which ran from Charleston to Keowee, a road also ran from the site west to Savannah River, making it popular for traders, trappers and hunters."[14]

Tales, territories, and terrains in North and South Carolina represented both internal and external struggles and challenges that often seemed impossible to conquer by man. Legends gave way to enlightenment and the ability to protect and love. Scaling of rough and rocky terrain of unexplored territories led to fertility, growth, protection and refuge in forests. The forceful beauty of waterfalls and the land carved out left patterns for others to view and follow. Valleys of peace and quiet surrounded by the mountains offered the opportunity for self-reflection as well as the opportunity for planting and sowing seed, thereby growing, multiplying and regenerating. No fear of hard work, the ability to weather storms, and the dominance of faith and love stand out loud and clear as traits essential for survival when born and raised in these areas, and they remain so today.

Chapter Three

A TALE OF TWO CAROLINIANS

JUST AS THE waterfalls in North Carolina and South Carolina connected to each other, complimented each other, and formed one long flowing forceful beauty of nature, so did the bonds of my grandparents. Just as the lands and people in North and South Carolina developed strong connections and important trails, so did my grandparents. These two people came together to create a story of their own. They developed it, defined it, refined it, and gave it a name.

Kansie Edna Whitmire Head was born in Transylvania County, North Carolina, on August 29, 1897. She was the daughter of Edward McDonald and Mary Emily Gillespie Whitmire. She had six siblings. They were Florence Olivia, Franklin Jordan, Annie Laura, Beulah, Walter Clyde, and Hassie Emily. Her sister Laura lived in Rosman where her son Vic and his wife Ella Mae later lived as well. My generation has memories of visiting with Vic and Ella Mae in Rosman. Granny graduated from Rosman High School which was 11 grades during her time. She worked in the Silversteen family store in Rosman, called The Gloucester Company Store. Granny's father was a farmer but was also the town magistrate for a period of time. She often helped her father with this endeavor, doing the paper work and such. Growing up in the mountains and working in the general store gave her experiences that served her well in her later years.

It is believed through ancestry family charts that the "Whitmire (Von Whittenmeyer) or Widmayer family was of German descent with family born in Enzweihingen, Wurttemberg, Germany in the 1700's. By 1774, family had moved to South Carolina. Whitmires would settle in Rosman, North Carolina, Whitmire, South Carolina and in North East Georgia. The Whitmires were apparently fond of expressing their loyalty and respect for famous people by naming their children after them. Second, third and fourth generations have sons named Christopher Columbus, George Washington, James Madison, Andrew Jackson and Napoleon Bonaparte Whitmire." [15] They either had lots of patriotism, respect for leaders, or a sense of humor that was passed down.

Ancestry family charts indicate that the "Gillespie family originally came from Scotland in the 1600's. Gillespie meant 'Servant of the Bishop,' and the Gillespie family furnished the Church of Scotland with some of its earliest ministers. As they arrived in America, they settled in Pennsylvania initially."[16] It was said that Granny was descended from a full-blooded Cherokee Indian possibly on her mother's side. Granny often told stories of seeing a family member in full Indian attire and colorful headdress who would visit. I have heard all of my life that Granny was part Cherokee, but I have not been able to validate that claim in any official capacity.

There is an interesting Civil War story centered on Crayton Gillespie, Granny's grandfather. He and his wife, Martha Easter Kennemur, had six children, one of whom was Kansie's mother, Mary Emily. "When he went off to fight in the Civil War, he left his wife and three little girls, promising he would return home safely and he would come home singing. Weeks after other Transylvania County men came home from the war, Crayton had not returned. It had been over a year since they had heard from him. One morning Martha was preparing breakfast and suddenly heard his voice, faint but steady as he limped along the road toward his house. Weak from illness that almost cost him his sight and from months in a Union prison, he had limped home slowly with the help of other soldiers.

Exhausted, hungry and dirty, he had come home-singing as he had promised."[17]

Granny's parents: Edward McDonald and Mary Emily Gillespie Whitmire

John Arthur Head was born in Salem, South Carolina, on February 4, 1897. He was the son of John Wesley and Mattie Elizabeth Rice Head. They had fifteen children. Five were born and died at a young age. They were Eddie, Gene Burley, Barney, Lela and Jim. Other children in addition to John Arthur included Lillie Maebell, Ollie Pearl, Tina Berline, Herbert Toy, Elbert Troy, Corrie, Alma Christine, William Eugene 'Buddy' and Ruby. Grandpa's mother, Mattie, would die from cancer in 1937. John Wesley would later marry Carrie Gentry. My aunts and uncles as well as siblings and cousins remember Berline and her son, Jerry. He was fondly called Sonny. They lived in Central and came to most of the family gatherings along with several others of Grandpa's siblings. Toy and his wife owned and operated a general store between Norris and Liberty. Elbert and his wife owned and operated a general store in Central.

It is believed from ancestry family charts that the "Rice family was of Irish and German descent and Mattie was an eighth generation descendant of a Lord Lieutenant of Ireland, Stephen Rice, whose son, Thomas, was later born in Bristol, England, and came to Virginia around 1680 aboard the Bristor Merchant. He was an apprentice to John Stephens in the UK before leaving on the ship. John Stephens was the captain. Later on in Thomas's life, he owned a small plantation in Virginia. He left his wife and children to return to England to receive a considerable estate that had been left to him. He did not return and sailors reported that he died at sea from what was thought to be an assassination in 1711. He nor his family ever received the property he had gone to claim." [18] Mattie was the daughter of a Baptist preacher and farmer. Her father had a brother that served as lieutenant in the confederate army.

Ancestry family charts indicate that John Wesley Head was a descendant of Alston Head, who was born in the early 1800's in North Carolina. [19] He was also a grandson of a Baptist preacher. He was affectionately called Gramps by the grandkids. The family is believed to have owned a grist mill and they farmed as well. He and his family lived in the Salem and Keowee area. According to authors Michael Hembree and Dot Jackson, the JW Heads owned land around the Shallow Ford area, near Nimmons Bridge, where the area was fertile and known for the crops it produced. [20]

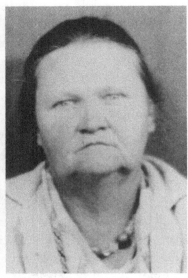

Grandpa's parents: John Wesley and Mattie Elizabeth Rice Head

Grandpa was drafted to serve in World War I. His basic training was near Greenville, South Carolina. He was never shipped overseas. As he was in Augusta, Georgia, waiting to be sent, the war ended. He also later served as an air raid warden in World War II. He made rounds at night to make sure people turned their lights off. If lights were seen on, he had to go and tell folks to turn them off. The government didn't want lights to be seen if the enemy flew over. His assignment included part of Central. Author Wilt Browning captures this event from the eyes of youth in his home of Easley, South Carolina. "There were those dark nights when 'blackouts' were staged, just to make sure that the light at our window did not lead some ... bomber in our direction in the event the war in Europe or the Pacific had gone bad for the Allies and fighting literally turned into a world-wide war. There was something unsettling about the exercise, but it was also like a game for the two of us preschoolers as we sat there, each trying to out-quiet the other."[21]

Grandpa told the kids stories about growing up in his day. Salem was not a big town and they would go to Walhalla to buy supplies or sell produce. They would travel by wagon to Walhalla. The travel would be a long adventure. Grandpa often told the boys of the trip being a two day event. They would go and camp overnight off of the Burnt Tanyard Road before returning. As Grandpa got older, he was able to make the trip by himself in the wagon.

The author Debbie Fletcher confirms the length of trips by wagon in, as she tells the story, of her granddaddy traveling by wagon from The Brown House Lodge (or Boarding Home) in the Keowee-Jocassee area to Seneca to pick up boarders who had arrived by train. "It was a full day to take the wagon into Seneca, and then he would spend the night and bring the trainload of people back to the Brown House. It would take another 12 hours to bring them all back." [22]

Grandpa told his sons about one time when he left Salem and went to Seneca. His plan was to hop aboard the circus train as it passed by. He got in an empty truck and stayed there until he heard the train coming. He managed to jump onto the side of the train as it passed by, and hung on for dear life. The door of the train car was locked, but after a few minutes, a man came and unlocked the door, not knowing anyone was hanging on the side. The man then went back to his seat. Grandpa was able to slide the door open and climb inside. Years later when telling his sons about the experience, Grandpa said "God saved my life that day because if the man had not unlocked the door, I would have fallen off and died."

Grandpa found his way to Maggie Valley and Rosman, North Carolina, in his young adult years to work. He worked in a lumber yard in Maggie Valley. He told his daughter, Lola, that while up on the mountain one day, the wind blew so hard that it blew his hat off and way down the mountain. It was at that moment he decided it was time to go home. Actually, one of his buddies died in a logging accident. It upset Grandpa so bad that he left for home and didn't even go back to get his paycheck. Later on he went to Rosman where he worked in a tannery. It is these early years that no doubt gave him training and experience for future business endeavors he would develop and manage. Grandpa had a third grade education, probably because of the farming needs of the family. Even so, he gained education in numerous other ways and became a very successful businessman.

Chapter Four

TWO BECOME ONE

IT WAS IN Rosman, North Carolina, where Grandpa met and married Granny. The story passed down has it that Grandpa first met Hassie, Granny's younger sister, and asked her for a date to a dance. Hassie told him that she was seeing someone else, but that she had a sister, Kansie, whom he should meet. He asked Granny for a date. The rest as they say is history. They married in 1922 in Rosman at Calvert Baptist Church and lived in Rosman until around 1924.

After Granny and Grandpa left Rosman, they moved to Central, South Carolina, and made their mark on a small town located half way between Atlanta, Georgia and Charlotte, North Carolina by way of train. It is believed that by this time, Grandpa's dad (Gramps) may have already moved to Central, thus making it one of the reasons they probably chose to live in Central. It is also believed that after the death of both of Granny's parents, a small inheritance from land sold afforded them the ability to venture out in some of their businesses. Her father died in August of 1926 and mother in November of 1926.

Central is the back drop for where Grandpa and Granny would live the rest of their lives, raise a family, establish businesses and impact many lives. The landscape of Central differed from the small isolated town of Salem and the booming mountain town of Rosman. It is ironic that the town they moved to was named Central. The word central means core, heart, base or forming the center; significant, of greatest importance, essential or principal. All of the terms are significant for raising a family and important as goals for making a difference and developing landmarks. The town of Central is located in Pickens County, South Carolina. "Pickens County was originally part of Cherokee territory until 1785 when it became part of the Ninety-Six Judicial District. It would be later divided into the Washington District in the late 1700s establishing the upstate of SC and composing present day counties of Greenville, Anderson, Oconee and Pickens in SC. The district was later divided into Greenville and Pendleton districts, with Pendleton encompassing Anderson, Oconee and Pickens counties as known today. The area would be divided again and called Pickens and Anderson districts. In 1868 the name districts were changed to counties and Oconee County was established out of part of Pickens County. Pickens County grew by the building of the Railway in 1870s with the towns of Central, Calhoun (Clemson), Liberty, Norris and Easley established due to the industry created."[23]

"Central was incorporated as a town on March 17, 1875, after The Atlantic and Richmond Air Line (Southern Railroad) had chosen Central to be the location for repairs, shops, a depot and railroad employee housing a couple of years earlier. A hotel was built and included a ticket office and waiting area as well as a restaurant. All was well with the town of Central in its early years until in the late 1890s, when the railroad moved the repair shops to Greenville. Everything changed. In addition to businesses closing, a fire broke out and destroyed a large portion of Main Street."[24]

A gleam of hope returned to Central in 1904 when Isaqueena Mill offered employment opportunities. "Pickens County's first cotton mill had been established in Cateechee in 1895. DK Norris came from that plant to help establish a new one in Central. Humble beginnings included kerosene lamps for lighting, outhouses for employee restrooms and steam engines and boilers powered the machinery."[25] Farming and now cotton mills would be the main sources of livelihood in those days in Central and aided in its rebirth.

Grandpa and Granny settled into living in the town of Central during its time of transition and contributed much to the town in the years that followed. Author Mattie Allen of *Central Yesterday and Today* devotes a chapter in her book to families who helped to advance the town of Central. She notes my grandparents in the section. "Mr. and Mrs. Arthur Head came from Rosman, North Carolina, in 1924 and ran a grocery store on Main Street. After this they bought land and built a number of rental houses. Here they operated a store and also manufactured cement blocks."[26] However, their impact on Central and their family was so much more.

They became the parents of nine children. The children in order of age included: Lois Edna, Lola Frances, James Arthur, Annie Laura, Johnny Ray, Paul Edward, Charles Elzie, Ernest Franklin and Doris Louise. In later years following Lois's death, they adopted her two children, Edna Lois and Reba Sue. Grandpa and Granny originally lived in a small red house close to a Roller Mill in town when they first moved to Central. That house was later used as an office and post office at various times for the town after they moved. Lois was born in Rosman before they moved, but their next four children were be born at this house.

Granny told a story to the kids of long ago when they were living in the little red house. Lois and Lola were the only two children at the time and both were little. Granny was outside and all of a sudden heard both girls screaming inside the house. She ran inside and asked Lois what was wrong. Lois replied, "Little baby was crying." There were also stories told of the kids playing outside and often hiding under the front porch for hide and seek and such.

Less than a mile away from the little red house, Grandpa would purchase land and build their forever home in 1934. Their new home was a four room house initially with a dining room, kitchen and 2 bedrooms. They later added on as more children were born. A front porch and a side porch, in addition to a front sitting room and bedroom were added. The front bedroom added was for Lois and Annie. That bedroom became a pivotal room in the home in years to come. They also extended and modified the kitchen and converted the side porch into a bathroom and storage room over time. The front porch was the foundation for many visits and talks with family and friends. The block house, complete with additions and renovations over time would total 7 main rooms plus a front porch that covered the entire front and part of the right side of the house. The house became the center of activity for the Head family. With their general store located directly across from it, and their block business and lumber mill close by as well, the area around their home became the hub for activity in the area. The house held many memories of the kids and grandkids. Lots of pictures were taken over the years of family members on the front porch or standing in front of the house in the yard. Pictures captured everyday occasions to Easter Sundays and other Sunday visits dressed in their best attire, with lots of happiness seen in the family pictures. From memories and photos, the house welcomed you with the big front porch and chairs streamed all along it, ending with a wooden swing on the far right side of the house if you were standing in front of it looking at it. Weather permitting, most of the family visits happened on the front porch. In order to enter the porch, there were five steps to climb. On both sides of the steps was a white wooden railing that extended the entire length of the porch. Below the railing was lattice work that covered the bottom half of the porch. The front of the house actually had two doors for entry. The main entrance welcomed you to the living room while the second door entered into a bedroom. When entering the living room, several framed photographs of family hang on the wall. To the right of the entry was a doorway that opened to the front bedroom. Coming back to living room, in the far right corner was a piano. On the left side of the room as you walked in, there was a couch located just below a window that looked out the side of the house. Leaving the living room and walking forward to the next room was the dining room. A large table was located on the left side of the room. Beside the table was a door that opened to the outside and a small porch. The porch connected to the well house. China cabinets surrounded the right wall of the dining room. Continuing forward from the dining room was the den that greeted you with warmth. It was the main sitting area. A television sat on a cabinet top and a couch and large chairs filled the borders of the room. To the left center of the room was a wood stove. As you passed the wood stove on the left you entered into the kitchen. On the left side of the room was a refrigerator, stove and cabinets which filled the wall. A small table filled the center of the room and on the immediate right side were more cabinets. In the right corner of the room was the back door that opened to the outside. To the left of the back door sat the sink, dryer and a dishwasher that was won from the hardware store, but never used. Back in the sitting room was also a door on the right side of the room. It entered into Granny and Grandpa's bedroom. In later years, a small room was added on to the side of their bedroom to make another small bedroom. From Granny and Grandpa's bedroom a doorway lead to what was called the middle bedroom. As renovations and add-ons were made, the side porch that originally extended the entire right side of the house was renovated into a bathroom and storage room, adjacent to the bedrooms. A door way located on the opposite side of the middle bedroom lead into the front bedroom, thus going full circle in the house. The kids concluded that was advantageous if one was hiding from someone. Doris told of a story when she was in trouble and Pa came looking for her. She heard the front door open and heard him coming in and calling her name. She was in the back of the house and took off into Granny and Grandpa's bedroom and ended up in the front of the house while he was making his way toward to the kitchen. She was able to escape out the front for a while until things calmed down. Thus the circular floor plan of the house had advantages.

Grandpa and Granny in front of their home in Central

This home would be a focal point in the lives of the Head children. Within it was found abundant memories of growing up, working hard, playing and many other activities surrounded in love. The family ate meals together and said grace before each meal. They worked together for common goals. They attended church together. They helped each other as well as their neighbors when someone was in need. Everyone trusted each other. No one locked their doors or feared their neighbors.

Charles remembers he would often be the one to get up and build a fire in the wood stove each morning as no other heat sources were available. Since winter nights could get really cold, they would often heat water on their wood burning stove and pour it into quart jars and close the lid. They would pull a stocking over it and then place it at their feet in the bed to warm them.

The boys told the story of the arrival of their baby sister Doris. The boys recalled they were sitting around the table playing some games, when Grandpa said "We are going to get the baby." Sometime later they came bringing in a baby from the bedroom. When one of the boys was asked what he thought about the new baby, he said "She shore has red hair" referring to his newborn sister, Doris.

Charles also fondly recalled reading the story of a beaver and a rabbit to a younger sibling. Charles read it so often that sometimes he would leave out some of the words and just repeatedly say bumpity, bumpity and thumpity, thumpity. After a few minutes it would be discovered that Charles was not reading every word in the book, so he would have to start over again and read the entire book word for word. In later years, Charles recalled a brother would pay him to cook Blair pudding. Blair was the brand name. If it had lumps in it, his brother would go to their dad saying that the pudding was lumpy and he wanted his money back. Grandpa would reply that he just had more pudding that way and he got more for his money.

John recalls as a youngster that the kids were given a nickel a piece for their allowance each week. Lois would take them into town to the store on Main Street in Central and let them get candy. A nickel would get them a bag of assorted or "messed up candy" as John would say.

Being able to go in to town or at least the outskirts was a big deal. Granny would have the kids to run errands on occasion. Granny sent Lola to the post office one day to mail some letters. There was a slot in the post office that read U.S. Mail. The slot was for outgoing mail to be placed. When Lola returned, Granny asked if she mailed the letters. Lola replied she "put them in the us mail slot."

Faith was a big part of Grandpa and Granny's life. Grandpa and Granny originally attended cottage prayer meetings in Central where people met in different homes each week to hold service. Later, they attended the Church of God of Prophecy in Central. Grandpa was instrumental in helping to build the church, supplying blocks and so on to help. As time progressed, they met a preacher who pastored a church in the Walhalla area after retiring from the mission field. Some of the family attended his church and revivals. After getting to know Grandpa, the preacher came to Central to help him to establish a church in Central, close to their home. Because of the many revivals to be held, it was named the Central Revival Center. They had various preachers and Grandpa often taught Sunday school. Granny played the piano and was the secretary-treasurer. Many homecomings were held on the grounds at the church with lots of people from the area attending. Family reunions and Christmas gatherings were also held there over the years. It seems that Grandpa somewhat followed in the footsteps of his grandfather and great grandfather who both were Baptist preachers and helped to establish several churches over their years. In those days, revivals lasted for two to three weeks at a time. Camp meetings were also big events. Those were held in Toccoa, Georgia, around the fourth of July. That date was popular because cotton mills always got the week of the fourth off, making it easier to attend. Those saved during the revivals would be taken on the back of a truck down to the lakes to get baptized.

In addition to church and homecomings, other community events such as fish fries were held in the area. Grandpa bought fish that would arrive by train from Ballard Fish and Oyster Company in Norfolk, Virginia. The order would be placed one day and it would arrive by noon the next day. It would still be covered with ice. Sometimes he would sell to the community and other times he would hold a large fish fry for the area. Those were always big hits. Meals would be prepared and often hundreds of people would join them in the fellowship. It was a great social event. The area and those who lived there worked together, played together and became a sense of family.

Many folks recall how when they had no money and were in need of food to feed their families, Granny would give them food from the store to get them through. Rent payments were often delayed several times in order to help people get back on their feet. On one occasion, Doris recalls when they went to a home to collect a house payment; the lady came to the door crying. Her husband had passed away, and she wasn't sure how she could pay them. Grandpa told her not to worry about it. He told Granny to write the lady a receipt for "Paid in Full" for the house. That would be one less worry for her. They gave her the house. This story was not surprising to many as their generosity was well known. Many people would not have ever owned a home if not for Grandpa. He gave fair pricing and a chance. He gave people jobs and a place to live. I think most of all he gave an opportunity and hope. The boys recalled that Grandpa often said; "giving to the poor is giving to the Lord."

"Blessed is he that considereth the poor: the Lord will deliver him in time of trouble."(Psalm 41: 1). "If there be among you a poor man of one of thy brethren within any of thy gates in thy land which the Lord thy God giveth thee, thou shalt not harden thine heart, nor shut thine hand from thy poor brother." (Deuteronomy 15:7)

Chapter Five

THE CENTRAL THEY KNEW

AS THE KIDS grew up, their stories and memories give a glimpse of Central and the way it was after my grandparents first relocated there. The train had taken its headquarters to Greenville, but the train was still viable for travel and shipping. Their business had moved from Main Street to closer to their home. Grandpa's father had a small store in town for a while but it had long closed as well. He moved into a house beside Grandpa and Granny and lived until his death in 1963. As some of their business ventures closed, new ones developed.

Around 1947 on Main Street in Central, a theatre was built. Grandpa was asked to make the blocks for it, but his business was not completely up and running at the time, so someone else made the blocks. There was a restaurant that connected to the theatre. A family ran the theatre and restaurant. The theatre was housed in a tent originally until the building was completed. Charles does remember that at the time, when the theatre was completed, it was a 2 story building. The Main Street would be covered with people going to eat or to the movies on the weekends. The shows were at 8 pm or 10 pm, and farmers from out of town would come. Everything closed at midnight. Stores opened at 5 am daily to accommodate farmers who may need to purchase something for their equipment and so on before getting started for the day and stayed open until midnight for them as well

Movies cost 25 cents per person in the 1950's. John and Clara would go to a movie on the weekend and each get a 25 cent hotdog. One dollar got them dinner and a movie. The young Head children were not allowed to go to the movies because at that time it was deemed a sin by their parents. John and his wife, Clara, took Doris and another brother to their first movie as they got older. Doris said she feared the entire time that she would be doomed to hell for going to the movie. She laughed as she told that story as times and beliefs had softened. As movies were frowned upon, so was television. Grandpa was not going to buy one. As luck would have it for the kids, Grandpa won one from the hardware store in Central. If a purchase of an appliance was made, a ticket was given to write down their name and put in a box for a chance to win a prize. Doris filled out the ticket and placed it in the box. Grandpa won a television. It was said to have taken all day for the folks to come out and install it. Grandpa also won a dishwasher that was never used at another drawing. As the kids remaining at home now had a television, they loved to watch cartoons and westerns. Doris said that as she and her brothers watched a western, it never failed that fighting among the cowboys only occurred when Grandpa walked into the room. Any other time, it would be calm. Grandpa must have thought for the longest time that westerns only included fighting. A cute story was told that even though a television was in the home, Grandpa did not think television was a good thing. One time he said that to someone in a conversation, and a granddaughter softly spoke out and said, but you watch *Felix the Cat*. I don't know if he heard the statement or not.

Charles laughed as he told a story about Grandpa's winning television. Charles was married at the time. Charles had met Ellen Hamilton at church services and later they married. He had bought appliances for their house, as well, and filled out tickets and gave them to a friend to put in the box at the hardware store. Later on, he found out they were placed in the wrong box as his name had been called for an electric skillet for another drawing, but the winner had to be present to win. When he heard that his name had been drawn, he laughed as that contest was different from the one for the television.

John said when he first got married that folks had to make a down payment of one third of the cost of the appliance before you could take it home. He laughed and said it took a while to get appliances needed for starting out in his marriage to Clara. Also, the availability of refrigerators and other appliances became more prevalent after World War II when rationing was eliminated. Before refrigeration in those days, ice blocks were sold in town. There was an ice house in Central on Main Street where the ice could be purchased and taken home or delivered. A nickel bought a block of ice about the size of a shoe box. A dime bought a block that was around 10 pounds, and a quarter bought a block large enough that a wagon was needed to deliver it. Sometimes they would cover the block in sawdust and it would insulate it enough to make it last for several days. I recall my mom, Annie, telling stories about large tins of lemonade that would be made and ice being chipped off from large blocks to keep it cold.

The arrival of the cotton mill in Central was a big addition for the town. To discuss the cotton mill in Central you have to discuss the one in Cateechee as well. "Colonel DK Norris came to the upstate of SC from Vance, SC, in the low country and built the first cotton mill in Pickens County in 1896. The mill was named after him and the town village that it was built in, he named Cateechee. It is believed that during his research of the twelve mile creek and land he acquired for the mill site that he came across the legend of the Indian Maiden Cateechee. As he later named the Central Mill Issaqueena (the other name for Cateechee) it is suggested he had a romantic spirit." [27] Issaqueena Mill in Central went into receivership during the depression, where court appointed control of the plant was given to an outsider to prevent bankruptcy, but it remained open and became Plant No. 12 of the Cannon Mills Company by 1950.[28]

When the cotton mills came to town, people didn't have clocks in their homes. The cotton mills would blow their whistles daily to alert workers that it was time to get ready for work. In Central, the whistle blew daily every morning at 5:30 am. It would blow twice to awaken everyone. At 6:40 am, it would blow again to alert folks that it was getting time for work, which started at 7 am. John worked in the mill for a few months. His job was to supply steam to cause the whistle to blow. According to author of *Red Hills and Cotton*, Ben Roberts, "At Cateechee Mill up the road, their whistle blew every morning at half past four in the morning and at six their shift work started. Their work hours were six am to six pm... Ben recalls when the mill first came, of sometimes lying in bed and waking up to hear the whistle blowing, long before daylight, and recalling how uneasy he felt... We ourselves got up before daylight, but there was something alarming in being ordered to rise by a factory whistle. It was the command that frightened...a sound that we had never heard before in our valley. He recalls how hard it was for folks to decide whether to give up the farm and outdoors for indoor work for sixty to seventy hours a week at times. I remember the problem they had to face when they decided to make the trade-to swap the furrow and the open for the cash of a daily wage. It was a hard life for some accustomed to the open, but Saturday was payday-every Saturday."[29] With the option of mill work, man was no longer dependent on the weather or pests that could interfere with a crop and thus their livelihood.

As cotton mills sprang up in the upstate, it became a way of life for many. Each of the mills developed their own unique community village. Employment in a mill usually became to mean living in a house built by the mill, having company stores and attending churches and schools specific to their area and community. Author, Branti Owens, describes the region and mill village as follows: "If this region were a piece of the fabric produced by local textile mills, each strand would contribute its unique quality to a cloth of strength, beauty and durability... a complex, living tapestry of the South Carolina experience: a deftly woven fabric of mountains, mills and memories."[30]

Wilt Browning writes the following statement in relation to losing the mill hill house once lived in by his family. "Mother and Dad now were gone and the house filled with so many memories soon would belong to someone I never knew... I fear that the old house, too, will show signs of yielding to the ravage of time, but I won't be there to mourn it. Still, someone ought to tell future owners how important that house really was. But so was every other house I now was passing. They all have history in their timbers, and ought to have historical markers out front." [31] Though he was referring to his childhood home in the mill village, this description covers most childhood homes. It does mine. My father worked at the Central Mill, from the age of sixteen until he retired at the age of sixty-two. In their early years of marriage and raising a family, my mom worked at Cannon Mills as well. My brothers had stints in the mill until they chose other professions. Cannon Mills would later become known as Central Textiles, but remains in business today. Even though we did not live on the mill village, we had a home built by my grandfather and uncles on a parcel of land in Central that my grandfather once owned. However, lots of those coworkers of my family members were wonderful friends to our family for many years and remain so today.

Emergency Services in Central were very limited. Charles recalled working one day at the saw mill when he noticed one of the houses on fire. He ran over to help and saw a man in the house on fire. He tried to help while someone went to call the funeral home for an ambulance. The man was transported to the hospital in Greenville. The story was intriguing for several reasons. Several of the boys later served as volunteer firefighters, and John later served as the Chief of the Central Fire Department for many years. Central would eventually have a rescue squad for several years that took over ambulance duties. Catching my attention also was the fact that the ambulance came from a funeral home. Ambulances were originally owned by funeral homes because hearses, large enough for caskets, also served for transport in emergencies as patients often needed to be able to lie down. Hearses served as both vehicles to transport coffins to funerals and to take sick and injured individuals to hospitals. These vehicles required just a few quick changes to serve one purpose or the other. "The ambulance business changed when new regulations on ambulance design and emergency medical care went into effect. In addition to these new standards, ambulance services also became very costly, forcing many funeral directors to give up the ambulance side of their businesses. Hospitals, fire departments, and private and volunteer operators took up the slack. By the late '60s and early '70s ambulances transformed from basic transport vehicles into mini mobile hospitals. This was partially due to the Vietnam War, which expanded trauma treatment and demonstrated that well-trained combat medics who didn't have medical degrees could save lives by providing on-the-spot care."[32]

The Graves Duckett funeral home was located on Gassaway Street in Central, across from the building that housed the switchboard for local telephone service. According to historian, Jerry Alexander, "Service area for both the telephone and ambulance service included Cateechee and Norris mill villages as well as Norris, Six Mile and Central. Even though telephones were very limited, the mill stores and offices as well as hotels had telephones for emergency use. Mr. Tom Folger owned the first telephone service in Central in 1931, called the Central Telephone Company and later became Southern Bell. There were 31 phones at that time. Mr. Folger also worked for the Norris Cotton Mill in various positions. All of the phone lines in that day were called party lines, meaning that several phones in the same area were given the same telephone line and each phone would have a given number of rings to denote their call." [33] With several households being on the same line, eavesdropping was probably pretty common.

The Heads tried several times to get a telephone from Mr. Folger and the company. They would always be put on a waiting list. After a period of time elapsed, they would ask again. John recalls that they were finally successful in getting a telephone at his expense. He had gone to Mr. Folgers along with Granny to make another request for a telephone. Mr. Folger's dog didn't take a liking to the visit apparently and bit John on the back of his leg. It was a pretty good bite that Mr. Folger witnessed. Granny got John home and the wound tended to and not long afterwards, the Head family had a telephone!!

Chapter Six

ALL IN A DAY'S WORK

IN ADDITION TO raising a family and developing a sense of community in the Central area, my grandparents were responsible for developing and operating multiple businesses. Grandpa developed a business for making cement blocks in 1946. The Jordan machine company from Orlando, Florida, brought a block making machine to Grandpa in Central. Blocks were sold for thirteen cents each. They could make a 6 inch or 12 inch size. Rock face blocks were made first. They made 6 blocks in one minute. It is believed they were the only business in the area to use that pattern. Those blocks were, and remain, very distinctive and easy to pick out as blocks made by the Heads on homes that are still standing today. Grandpa would also purchase a block mill out of Pickens and would later buy another block mill from a business in Central. That business owned another small business in Pendleton and later sold it to my grandfather. He kept it in Pendleton for a month or so and then moved it to Central. Charles said that Grandpa improved upon the machines once he got them. A tweak here or there would make it faster, sturdier, etc. Grandpa was a fixer. If something broke, he often found ways to fix it or replace it with something better and more efficient. Working in the businesses was hard work and pretty much all manual labor. No fancy technology or computer apps were available to help measure, weigh, cut or make the materials. Neither was there much fancy equipment to use. Everything was done by hand. Sand was pumped out of the creek bed from Eighteen Mile Creek.

They would shovel and load truckloads of sand from the creek to be brought back, unloaded from the truck and then used in the making of blocks. Once made, the blocks then had to be delivered.

John and Charles told of a story when they received an order for 2,000 cement blocks from someone in Calhoun Falls, around 60 miles away. Their one available truck could only hold about 500 blocks. John, Charles and a coworker, Mose, loaded the truck the night before and then started out early the next morning, taking turns driving. They made a total of 4 trips to Calhoun Falls that one day, each load delivering 500 blocks, until all 2,000 were delivered. They laughed and said that sure made for one long tiring day. This story, however, goes to show they did whatever they had to do to get a job done. John stated that he was sure he had hauled over a million blocks in his lifetime. They delivered blocks all around the upstate and even to Rosman to help build their aunt Hassie's store. Story had it that once they were delivered to Hassie, she helped to lay the block, but no one has been able to confirm or deny that report.

John also shared a story about one time hauling blocks in the mountains when their truck got hot and they pulled over for a rest in front of a house. A man came out and talked to them. Before they left, the man had ordered a load of blocks from them. John laughed because at the time, they didn't get any prepayment or even get the man's name. He just knew where he lived. They later delivered the blocks and the man paid them. A man's word sure had a different value in those days. Well, it has the same value, but the integrity behind it isn't the same today.

In addition to making blocks, two sawmills were owned and operated by Grandpa. He had one saw mill in Toccoa, Georgia, and the lumber came from the timber cut on Currohee Mountain. Mr. Bell managed and ran the saw mill. He would return to Central on the back of a mule if he came home on weekends and such, as well as when the mill closed and he returned home for good. The other sawmill was located in Central close by the block business. A lot of that timber was obtained in West Union. White Pine was made into various sizes of lumber. Once the lumber was cut, John said that he would lay it in the pig pen, placing it in a criss cross or lattice work pattern over the edges of the pen, for the wood to dry. Grandpa did have one special piece of equipment that could shape the sides or ends of the lumber in such a way as to work like "tongue and groove action" which connected the pieces together. This lumber was used for flooring. John usually ran the saw and Charles was responsible for keeping the boiler hot so that steam could move the pulley on the machinery and keep the lumber moving.

Making blocks and lumber seemed to naturally lead to building houses. Grandpa built many houses and businesses in various local places over the years. Some of those buildings are still standing in Central and the Pendleton area today. John says they probably built over 300 houses during their building days. Houses cost $1,200. They were small by today's standards, consisting of around 4 rooms, but Grandpa helped a lot of people get started living in their own home they otherwise could not have afforded. People purchasing the house would make a down payment of around $5 or whatever they could afford. Then they would make weekly payments until they were able to pay the debt in full. They usually paid $5 or so a month, again whatever they could afford. Every Saturday was payment collection day, where Granny and Grandpa would go to the homes and collect payments.

In addition to the new home owners, Grandpa built rental houses for a large population in the area where they had built their own home, and the area fondly became known as Head Town. The 14 acres of land consisted of their home, a saw mill and a building for making blocks, a general store, a church and rental houses. Around 40 houses were built and rented out or given to employees to live in as they worked for Grandpa. If you came to work for him, you had a house to live in. This was very similar to how the mill villages, such as the one in Central worked as well. If you worked for the mill, you had access to a house to live in. The same principle existed with Grandpa. As the kids grew up and married, they started out in a house close by in Head Town. This was usually where they lived as they started out in marriage and had children. Later several of the kids and their spouses purchased property from Grandpa on the out-skirts of the town and would have their home built. Several of those homes are still standing today with grandchildren living in them.

After their move to Central, Grandpa and Granny originally operated a general store in West Union as well as one on Main Street in Central. Grandpa ran the store in West Union and Granny ran the one on Main Street. The Depression would hit them hard and lead to the closing of those businesses. They owned and operated a small store right bedside their home for a period of time until they built a larger one across from their home.

In 1947 they built and ran the general store across from their home. Harold Hawkins, husband of their daughter Lola, helped to build it after he got out of the military. He laid the blocks and helped with the electrical wiring. The small white store had the block face design and sat in an easily accessible location for the folks in the area. In front of the store on the right side was a gas pump where gas was sold by the gallon. There were no increments or decimals on the pump like there are today. On the left side of the store in front was a drink box holding bottles of ice cold soft drinks. There was a pump there as well for dispensing kerosene. A shingle roof painted green covered the top of the store. Lots of memories of that store remain today with many of the grandchildren. The kids and some of the grand kids even worked in the store. It was a rock for the community as well. A small area in the back was designated for Granny's office. That is where Granny ordered blocks, lumber, and so on.

In the front of the store on the right side as you entered was another drink box holding bottles of soft drinks. In the right corner sat a roll top desk. To the left of the drink box and desk sat a wood stove to heat the area. A rocking chair sat between the desk and wood stove. A couple of wooden crates sat around on the floor as well to serve as a seat if someone had a couple of minutes to spare and visit. Beyond the wood stove and against the wall were shelves that held various parts for tractors and various tools. Further down the wall on the shelves were various pairs of shoes or other items that Grandpa purchased from a salesman. In front of the wall was a candy counter. The top and front of it was glass so that one could see the various types of sweet treats that it held. The back of the counter had a door that slid open and closed. Small bags sat on top of the counter, and you could fill it with any type of the candy for five cents a bag. The counter top extended further down the row and became a wooden top to hold items ready to be rung up for sale at the cash register. Brown paper bags in two sizes sat on the counter for bagging grocery items purchased. On top of Granny's register, she had some metal files with patron's names on it. As most everyone purchased items on credit, she could fill out their purchase and place a slip of the paper with the amount owed into the person's file. As they came in to make payments, she could update the information. It was also in this back corner of the store area where Granny had her office, so to speak for lumber and block purchases. Shelves of canned foods formed the center aisle just in front of the main entrance. Immediately on the left side of the shelves of canned food at the front was a bread rack. Three glass jars with lids sat on top held individual packs of various crackers and cookies. The racks beneath the top shelf held loaves of bread and individual snack cakes for sale. On the immediate left side of the store as you entered was an ice cream box. As you opened the lid, you could see a variety of ice cream snacks such as orange sherbet push-ups, ice cream sandwiches and cones. On the far left wall were more shelves holding tools and so on. Under those shelves sat a produce table and further down the aisle was a counter with scales and a paper rack for weighing and wrapping meat once purchased. Behind the counter sat two refrigerators containing a variety of meats. Further down the aisle lead to double doors that took you outside. Around the corner were more shelves lining the back wall. Buckets of syrup that had been made were available for purchase. Along with the syrup they had made, there were cans of green beans they had grown in the garden and canned at the cannery just above the street in Central. In front of those shelves was another counter. Beside the counter sat flats of eggs. The counter held a meat slicer, a cleaver and hoop cheese. Hoop cheese was a creamy type of cheese that was placed in a round mold and usually had a red wax around it. Granny had some clients who could not read. When they came into the store, she would walk around with them to help them get the groceries they needed. Some would send a list to the store for Granny to bag the items up for them and pick them up at a later time. One lady had written down soap, so Granny placed a bar of soap in the bag. Later on the lady came back and said that she had given her soap and she hadn't asked for it. After a little discussion, she had wanted some hoop cheese. That spelling was just a tad bit off. Another lady loved the cheese. She always came in and asked for a slice of the "whoop" cheese. Granny believed that they gave people "good prices" on everything. That is probably one main reason the store was in business from 1947 until it closed around 1972 when Granny turned 75.

As some of the grandchildren grew up and wanted to work, they would be given jobs. On collection Saturdays, Annie's oldest son, David, and one of Lola's daughters, Joanne, worked while Granny and Grandpa made their routes for collecting payments. From about 10 am until 2pm, they covered the store. David remembers pumping gas for seventeen cents a gallon. Some of the family worked in the store other times as well, including granddaughter Margaret and son-in-law Roger. Joanne and others recalled how Paul worked in the store when he was able. He took a lot of pride in keeping the store organized. He always swept the floors, dusted the shelves and kept everything meticulously in place.

They used various vendors for products to sell. An oil company from Pickens delivered gasoline. A salesman would come by weekly and Granny would give them an order and then later the supplies would be delivered. Doris recalls one time a man brought an order of crackers and cookies in and took them to the back of the store. Granny told Doris to go and find out how much they owed and give him the money. Doris asked him and he told her "sixty-nine." She replied sixty-nine dollars? He laughed, "No" he said, "sixty-nine cents."

Granny was the numbers person and brains behind it all. She managed all of the orders and bills for all of the businesses. She handled all of the money. One could say the little office in the store was the center of all activity, especially on paydays. When the boys worked for the family businesses, they were paid a salary. They worked 7am to 6pm with one hour for lunch Monday through Friday and 7am to noon on Saturdays. Their salary was around $20 a week when they first started. Salary negotiations usually occurred with Grandpa. Granny gave out the pay each week. There was not a lot of extra cash in the day. Every available dollar went back into the business or for paying salaries and such. It is important to note that the work hours were in addition to the normal chores they were assigned as well. Thus, sunup to sundown was no joke.

As one can imagine with so many businesses, there were a variety of people outside of the Head family that would be employed in helping and leave fond memories with the family. One of their coworkers was a man named Charlie. He was a carpenter and part time preacher. When building the houses, sometimes the frame would not be level. The boys would often go behind him and fix it. One day Charles mentioned this to Charlie, and Charlie slid a shim under a piece of wood to make the frame look level. Charles questioned him, wondering if that fix would hold up and last. Charlie replied, "the man on the riding horse won't know the difference." He meant that the house would look fine and level from a distance. It would only be on a close inspection that you could see a difference. This became a saying in the Head family that has stood the test of time, as did the houses. Charlie also smoked Fatima cigarettes. Charles told him they were bad for him and Charlie just replied, "Something has kept me here." Mose has already been mentioned as in helping to haul blocks. He helped out in a variety of ways wherever needed. Another worker was named Raymond. He lived in a house close to Grandpa and Granny and he worked for Grandpa. The kids always tried to find ways to aggravate and tease him. When the family prepared meals, they always fixed enough for Raymond to eat as well. One day, in between meal time, Raymond decided he was hungry and told Grandpa. Grandpa found Doris and told her to go fix Raymond something to eat. Doris was busy and didn't want to be bothered at the time, but knew she was to do as she was told. She made Raymond a peanut butter sandwich and added some flavor by putting soap in it and covering it with the bread. Raymond took one bite and started hollering, "Mr. R, Mr. R, they feeding me soap!!" R was short for Arthur. Another time they played tricks on Raymond by taking a mail order catalog and cutting out the name "Marshall Fields." They would put the name on a mound of dirt in Raymond's yard and add an old flower they had found to make a grave in his yard. Raymond would see it and take the flowers and name off. The kids would go back and put the name back down and add flowers. One day, after the second or third "funeral", Raymond had enough and ran to Grandpa. "Mr. R, Mr. R, they are burying the dead!!" Still another occasion, Charles knew Raymond was scared of snakes. Charles came across a small one and wrapped it on the end of a stick. He saw Raymond and started chasing him with it. I am sure he started hollering "Mr. R, Mr. R." Poor Raymond. He was afraid of most everything and playing tricks on him was the fondest form of friendship and flattery. I am sure he played a few tricks on them as well from time to time. There were several other workers with varying responsibilities as well as personalities. They were too numerous to mention all of them.

In addition to the land he owned in town, Grandpa purchased land in multiple locations in Central out of today's city limits. Several of their children over time would build homes on the parcels of land. Grandpa owned over 400 acres of land at one time. With accrual of all of the land, farming became a big part of their life as well. Cotton fields, sugar cane, wheat and corn could be found growing and needing to be harvested. He was also a cattle farmer. At one time he had around 150 head of cattle. Part of one of the areas and road would be named Heads Lake Road. If you are wondering about the name Heads Lake Road, you would be correct to assume a lake was around. From some of the natural springs on the land, he had 2 lakes created and connected by a damn. One was referred to as the upper lake or pond and the other was the lower one. Around the damn was an old waterwheel as well that circled for many years. He had the lakes stocked with catfish and carp fish from a fish hatchery in North Carolina, and then opened a business for fishing. Folks could buy tickets to fish for 2 hours at a time. They built a small block building and sold fish bait of minnows or worms, as well as cold soft drinks, crackers, candy bars and cookies. My brothers have fond memories of fishing and enjoying those cookies. My cousin, Joanne, recalled fond memories of her and her dad, Harold Hawkins, getting up early and going to the pond to fish. She recalls she used a cane pole as a fishing rod. She recalled the two of them would sit there for hours in the quietness and just fish. She also remembered purchasing a drink and especially candy bars from the store. The "Zero" candy bars were her favorite. Granny or Mrs. Bell usually operated the store. My brother, David, had a friend to tell him many years later in life about visiting his grandpa's fishing pond. He said he asked the lord for forgiveness for his actions. One day he and a buddy snuck into the lake area and fished for a while without buying a ticket. They caught a bucket full of fish and then headed home on foot. As they were walking up the road, Grandpa was driving by and saw them and stopped. He asked the boys what they were doing and they told him they had been fishing. He asked if the fish came from his pond. They said "no." They said they had been fishing in Eighteen Mile Creek which was close by. He asked if they were sure about that and they said, "yes." They talked for a few minutes and before leaving, Grandpa had bought the bucket of fish from the boys for fifty cent and took them and put them back into the pond as they were still alive. The friend laughed about his mischievousness. Their story gave catch and release a new meaning for sure.

Most all of the roads were dirt when the kids were growing up. A scraper would be attached to the back of a tractor and pulled around to smooth the road out as much as possible. Charles stated that during their childhood, there were two paved roads. One was the thoroughfare along Main Street that ran from Atlanta to

Charlotte and another road that ran from Central to Highway 88 in Pendleton. The layout of the roads changed as the original road that is now along Eighteen Mile Creek ran closer to Heads Lake road of today. Several acres of Grandpa's land were acquired in the early 1960's to make way for a new Highway 123 that linked Clemson to Easley, as the new planned highway ran through some of his property. Grandpa referred to the land in the area as the bottoms and planted large cornfields in that area surrounded by creeks and streams. His cattle also roamed on part of the land. When the land was purchased and road paved, a culvert was placed under the road. This space under the road gave the opportunity for cattle to go under the highway to get to either side for water and grazing. "SC Highway 93 today was the original alignment of US 123 from Clemson to Easley and when US 123 was given a bypass to the south of Easley in 1958, it became US 123 Business. When this project was finished, all of former US 123 from Easley to Clemson was renumbered as today's SC 93. "[34] Prior to improvements in the roads of the upstate, most were built upon old Indian trails, which pursued a straight course (up one hill and down another) without any respect for grade whatsoever. The grade became an issue because fuel and water pumps were placed near the top of a car engine. If the road was too steep of a climb, fluid could not flow and the car would not run.

One additional business adventure that Grandpa was involved in was mica mining. He had mica mines in two locations for a period of time. Some family members remember pieces of the mica being packaged in boxes and then sold in Spruce Pines, NC. An article published in 1953, "Mica Deposits of the Southeastern Piedmont, Part seven and eight" listed Grandpa's mine in the survey and looked at the distribution and structure of pegmatite bodies in the areas, their mineralogical characteristics, and the economic possibilities of the mica and other minerals. The article suggests that most of the mining in the area probably occurred in the early to mid-1940's and was done by breaking down rocks with picks and moved with shovels, wheelbarrows, buckets and the use of winches to hoist weighted materials. [35] Grandpa's deposit, called" the Head Prospect, was located 0.7 miles northwest of Twelve Mile Creek and 4 and 1/4 miles north of Clemson College."[36] At some point during his mining venture, he decided the mining was no longer safe and advantageous so he closed the mines down. It is unknown if he owned the land where they were located or had some type of business arrangement. This was just one more facet of this business man.

In an article written by Paul Clark and published in the *Smoky Mountain Living Magazine*, he tells us of " the relationship between mica and Spruce Pine, North Carolina, nicknamed "The Mineral City." The nation's mica mining activity was centered there in the late 1800's. Because of the region's mountains (some of the oldest in the world), North Carolina is the nation's leading producer of mica, that glass-like material most kids collected and peeled apart ... used in cosmetics, roofing felt, shingles, car paint, plastics, and wallboard.... A mica boom, begun in the mountains in 1878, helped supply materials for an insulator in Thomas Edison's electric motor."[37]

An excerpt from author, Ben Robertson, in *Red Hills and Cotton: an upcountry memory*, caught my attention and includes the following: "Sometimes, I think we are like the Blue Ridge Mountains- we are a Southern range of granite with monolithic peaks like our grandfathers, but all about these peaks are hundreds of fallen rocks and flimsily wedged boulders, glowing and glistening and flecked with mica and warm in the sun."[38]

Just like the mica, my grandparents had small pieces or flecks of courage, insight, ingenuity and determination that lead to the development of landmarks. Not always done in grandeur, sometimes unnoticed and seemingly having little value at times, they made a solid, steady and lasting mark, served a purpose and fulfilled a destiny when given the opportunity.

Chapter Seven

GRANNY

MUCH IS NOTED about Grandpa and the business ventures he created. His ingenuity, forward thinking and ability to make things happen speaks for itself. But it is the matriarch of the family that also wore many hats, juggled many ventures, and kept the family together. From handling business transactions, helping others and providing motherly love, she managed it all with even temperament and the ability to laugh as well. The statement, "Behind every good man is a good woman" could be no more accurate than describing the relationship between Grandpa and Granny.

As Granny had a reputation for her expertise with numbers, there was a professor from Clemson that came to her and asked her if she could help him. He came and bought lumber from the mill and was impressed with her mathematical skills. He taught math and wanted her to show him how she calculated numbers with such expertise. He also pleaded with her to tell no one!!! Granny calculated lumber needed in two ways. If she calculated in board feet, an eight feet board that was twelve inches wide was eight feet. If the board was only 6 inches wide, it was 4 feet to get her numbers. If she calculated in linear feet, an eight feet board was eight feet regardless of its width. She calculated a project down to the exact number of pieces of lumber or the number of blocks needed.

Granny loved crossword puzzles and was expert in completing them, in ink no less. Doris tells of a young man who delivered papers and would stop by the store every day. He would leave his backpack with papers on his bike parked in front of the store and go to watch the blocks being made, leaving his newspapers unattended. Granny would pick one up, complete the cross word section then return the newspaper back to his backpack while smiling all the way. Wonder what the recipient of that newspaper thought when he/she got a paper which already had the crossword puzzle completed, and in ink?

Granny also loved to crochet. She made lace that could be sewn onto pillow cases, towels and such to decorate them. She crocheted small crosses that were bookmarks for the Bible. She made her own caps that she wore year round. She also loved aprons and wore them almost all of the time. They always had big pockets so that she could keep any essentials she might need. I recall she kept a pen and pad of paper in it. I am sure that came from running the store and needing to have paper handy for writing notes or receipt book for record keeping. In her day, aprons were a part of fashion and served many purposes. As the number of dresses one had was very limited, and laundry a tedious job, keeping dresses as clean and covered as much as possible helped to extend the life of the dress. Aprons also served as excellent pot holders when cooking, assisted in cleaning a dirty spot, a small spill or dusting a piece of furniture. They worked for wiping sweat from the brow and were very handy if you needed to carry several items at one time.

Granny wearing one of her hats and apron.
Displaying a new crocheted hat she had made

Granny handled all of the money. When she opened bills it would say, "Please remit" whatever amount of money was owed. Doris recalls Grandpa looked at the bills one time and asked "Who is Plez Remit?" as he appeared on all of the bills. Granny smiled and explained.

Granny also helped the children with their homework from school, when needed. Charles recalled that Granny taught him a mnemonic to help him learn how to spell geography: George Earle's Oldest Girl Rode a Pig Home Yesterday.

Granny's father was a farmer and owned property on both sides of the French Broad River in Rosman. Their house sat next to the river and they kept a fish basket in the river. Whenever they wanted fish, they would go and pull fish out from the basket. She told the boys she didn't like doing that because you couldn't see in the basket and was afraid of pulling a snake out. That fear of snakes ran in the family and was passed down for generations. She was also familiar with wildlife and cooking game. One of her sons described her as a "mountain woman. She is the one who taught us about squirrels, rabbits and possums." Even though she was educated, she knew her roots and was tough when she needed to be.

Granny told the kids stories of when she was pregnant with her first child, Lois. Her brother Jordan lived close by. He would always sneak around and bring her food that she shouldn't be eating. He would bring her snacks and goodies. John also had fond memories of Jordan. He mailed John a Christmas card one year, and it had a one dollar bill in it for a Christmas present. John was so proud of receiving it and remembered that act of kindness many later years down the road. Granny's brother Walter often visited. The kids had fond memories of his visits and were always playing tricks on him. Apparently one time when their Uncle Walter was visiting and fell asleep, some of the boys wiped opossum grease around his lips and hands. When Walter woke up and saw the grease, he laughed when the boys told him it was "possum" grease, and he said he must have eaten some of that "possum" that he thought he had refused. When one of Granny's sisters was courting a fellow from out of town, he would usually wind up staying overnight in their house in an extra bedroom during his visits. The kids being as welcoming as one could imagine, would always play tricks. One night before the boyfriend went to bed, they had taken an old tire rubber and placed it in the creek water to get it good and cold. They snuck in and put it at the foot of his bed under the covers before he retired. When he got into the bed, he started screaming "Snake, Snake!!!!" He thought the biggest snake in the world was in his bed. On one other occasion, the kids put pine cones in his bed. When he went to get in the bed, he went to hollering!!! I can almost see my Granny grinning as she recalled the stories. She was a prankster and I am sure she was in the middle of those pranks and more.

Granny's father was also the town magistrate for a period of time. She often helped her father with this endeavor, doing the paper work and such. One time her father was away from the house when a man came that needed a bond set and paper work completed. They knew he was to come that day, but he came early. Granny talked to the man and set a fee. Her father came back as she was completing the process and finished with the man. Afterwards, Granny's mother told her she could not do such in her father's absence. Granny just shrugged and said, "He was guilty and I knew what daddy would have set the fee for." She didn't see it to be an issue. She had it under control.

Granny was an expert piano player who never took formal lessons. A piano teacher came and taught her older sister how to play. As the lessons were being given, Granny stood outside the door and listened. As soon as the session was over and the teacher left, Granny would enter the room, sit at the piano and play what was taught at that session. Her sister would get upset and tell their mom, "Make her quit. She is in there playing what I am playing."

Granny was a critical part to the success of the Head family, not only in business, but the children they raised. The scripture of 2 Timothy 1:5 comes to mind. "When I call to remembrance the unfeigned (genuine) faith that is in thee, which dwelt first in thy grandmother Lois, and thy mother Eunice; I am persuaded that is in thee also."

Granny had several relatives with colorful history. Granny's grandfather, Crayton Gillespie, who in addition to serving in the Civil War was a descendent in the long line of gunsmiths in the area around Rosman. Crayton was the grandson of William Gillespie. "Pennsylvania gunsmith, John Gillespie, and his wife moved to South Carolina from Virginia and then later settled in North Carolina around the East Fork area of the French Broad River. He built a gun shop. The Gillespie Rifle was known as 'the most accurate gun in the world'. The rifle had a smaller bore and longer barrel making it more successful than any of its predecessors. Daniel Boone's gun that he called 'Bess' was thought to have been a Gillespie made rifle" writes Susan Lefler[39]

Excerpts from stories in ancestry.com including "The Gillespie Gun Makers of East Fork NC" by Dennis Glazener, tell the following story:

> John and Jane Gillespie had six children, three sons and three daughters. John taught his sons, William, Matthew and Robert the trade and began making what is today known as the Gillespie Long Rifles. Even though all three sons knew the gun making business, the middle son Matthew and his family became the most famous.
>
> Gillespie rifles were muzzle-loaders where the powder was first put through the barrel and then wadding packed down in the barrel and then the greased bullet wrapped in cloth was pushed in. The rifle had to be reloaded after each shot in order to shoot again. The guns were made by hand, so each gun had its own specific bullets made to go with it. Walnut or maple wood were shaped with tools into the stocks which were characteristic of these rifles. The long barrels of the rifles were made from wrought-iron bars. Several bars were clamped around a small rod and welded together by a protracted process of repeated heating and hammering. It is believed that John purchased the iron needed to fabricate their rifles from Philip Sitton's iron forge at South Mills River in Henderson County. He would send his son Matthew to get the iron. Matthew met his daughter Elizabeth and they were married. Matthew's sister, Isabel Gillespie, would later marry Lawrence Sitton, a son of Philip Sitton. Mathew decided to establish his own gun shop at South Mills River near the iron works of his wife's family. He became known as one of the best known rifle makers around. He and Elizabeth became the parents of five sons and seven daughters. Their sons followed

in their father's and grandfather's footsteps by learning the skill of gun making. Each of them inscribed their initials and the year on the rifles as they were finished. No two were the same, but one could be spotted anywhere. Every man wanted one. It is said that when men from Henderson County went off to the Civil War, many were carrying a Gillespie rifle. It is said the Gillespie long rifles became a frontier legend and even created some as well as a few myths. It is not known how many Gillespie rifles were made, but a number of them have been preserved by collectors or descendants of the gun makers. "The advent of breech-loading and repeating rifles essentially ended the era of Gillespie style cap-and-ball, muzzle-loading rifles. However, in a concession to tradition, a special one-week season for deer hunting restricted to muzzle-loading rifles or shotguns is still scheduled each hunting season in some states.... Of course, most of the weapons used in these hunts have been modified to increase the accuracy and convenience of reloading as compared to the Gillespie rifles made before 1860. Matthew and Elizabeth's son Harvey died in the Mills River area in 1877. Two sons, John and James ran gun shops in Blairsville, Georgia, and then John moved to Young Harris, Georgia, until their deaths in the mid to late 1890's. Two other sons, Phillip and Wilson, died during the war in 1863.[40]

"The long line of gunsmiths would total 15 different craftsmen producing "thousands of Gillespie muskets and rifles up until the late 1890s explains Glazener. John Harvey Gillespie, who died in 1891, probably made the last Gillespie rifle.[41]

Another story centers around Philip Gillespie, known to be a mountain legend of sorts in his parts according to stories in ancestry. com. "He acquired a title to 347 acres of land on South Mills River in 1849. The property had originally been part of a 3,000 acre bounty grant from the state to Philip Sitton as an incentive to establish his iron forge. In addition to his gun making, Philip Gillespie farmed and operated a fruit distillery. He became the subject of local legend when he is supposed to have hidden a cask of his brandy and some gold coins prior to leaving Mills River in August 1863 to join Union forces in Tennessee. He died near Maynardsville, Tennessee, in January 1864, apparently without leaving instruction on the location of his treasure. Since then, many have searched for Philip's brandy and gold but if anyone was successful, they have not claimed credit."[42]

Chapter Eight

HARVEST TIMES

WITH THE TALENT, skills and ingenuity in the bloodlines of both Grandpa and Granny, it comes as no surprise that they were successful in most of their business endeavors. Each of their strengths and weaknesses appeared to complement each other and strengthen their relationship. When thinking about all of their endeavors, it appears they took advantage of any opportunity that came their way and they made the most of it. With many of the businesses, there was a time for sowing, but also a time for harvest. For farming ventures, crops had to be harvested. Cotton was picked and then sold for manufacturing endeavors. Corn was gathered and preserved in various ways including made into corn meal. Wheat was harvested from the fields and made into flour, and molasses made from sugar cane. All of these were common endeavors in the Head family. Both the sons and daughters were often involved in harvesting ventures.

When the sugar cane was ready for harvest, the process began with cutting the cane stalks down with a tractor and then going back and cutting the heads off of the stalks by hand. It would cause many cuts and scratches on a body as the stalks were hard with prickly parts as Lola attested to in one story. John fondly recalled one incident where after cutting the cane down, he had to do something before getting back to help Lola cut the heads off. When he returned, she was frustrated and told him "You just took your time to get back here to get out of work while I was here bleeding to death." Once the cane was harvested, it was taken from the farm back to their home and behind the store. There was a little shed set up with vats to pour the cane in to make the molasses. The vats had rocks under them and a fire would be started under the vats and the cane placed in them and brought to a boil. Once the pomace or juice from the cane boiled, it would be stirred and moved toward the front of the vat as it thickened to where a spout was located that could be opened to release the now syrup into large containers. This process took around 30 minutes. Bees liked the juice. The boys recalled numerous times running around in bare feet dodging bees, but still getting a few stings. Hogs and cows liked the juice as well. They were fed the remains of the juice and they would consume it until they got sick or tipsy, even though it wasn't fermented. After the syrup was harvested from the vats, it would be taken into the house through the front door and into the kitchen. Apparently it would spill out and drain a little along the way. The syrup clung to everything and it got everywhere. It is understandable that Granny often complained after batches were made. "The whole house is sticky" and of course, extra house work was needed. Once made, the sugar cane molasses were placed in quart size aluminum buckets with a lid and packaged for sale. Along with some of the kids, Guy, a friend of the family, helped to sell it. Guy would sample it in front of folks, proclaiming how good it was and folks would buy it. Some would be sold at their store as well.

Charles laughed as he recalled one time when he, his brother and Mose, a family friend, went to the mountains to sell some of the syrup. In one of the stores, Charles saw Clemson Blue Cheese for the first time and bought some. He had heard so much about the famed blue cheese and was excited to taste it. When he opened it, they all took one look and sniff and declared it was molded and ruined!!! Obviously they had not had blue cheese before.

The famous "Clemson Blue Cheese was developed by a Professor at Clemson A&M for a research project in 1940. Clemson would be named as a University in 1964. The interior of the vacant Stump House Mountain tunnel, once home to the Blue Ridge Railroad, was thought to be ideal temperature and moisture for curing blue cheese. After purchase by Clemson A&M College, the vacant tunnel housed cheese curing equipment by the Clemson College Dairy Department. World War II and issues surrounding ownership of the tunnel hampered development for several years. When Newman Hall at Clemson was built in 1956, the process was eventually moved back to campus for year round manufacturing. Clemson Blue Cheese is an artisan cheese made in large vats yielding around 240 pounds that becomes salted, waxed and aged for six months." [43] It remains a popular item today.

Along with sugar cane, growing and harvesting cotton and hay were big as well. I remember a story my mom, Annie, told many times related to picking cotton. The field was right beside their house and her four boys would pick cotton. I had not even been born as of yet. The boys were each to fill a bag full of cotton and they were paid depending upon the weight of the bag. Annie remembered one day, close to quitting time, being in the field to check on the boys. The three older boys, David, John, and Cecil had their bags almost full and were finishing up. She found the youngest son, Tom, sleeping in the field. He had fallen asleep and not picked any. She told how she woke him up and they scurried around to get him a bag of cotton to be weighed. She would always laugh when she would tell the story and say, "He was just a little bitty thing at the time. Probably could barely walk. " Hot summers were always full of the sons and grandsons helping to cut and bale hay for feeding the cattle later on. Long, hot, sweaty days fostered lots of memories, not all of them fond ones, but certainly instilled a valuable work ethic.

The farm did, however, foster fond memories for several of the grandchildren as they recall how Grandpa and sometimes Granny would take evening drives from in town to go over to the farm to check things out. It was almost like clockwork when they would appear driving along the roads and waving when they saw everyone. One could say a harvest of memories remains even years later among the family.

When one thinks of harvest, it could also be related to gathering or collecting of something of value from a service provided or granted. The Head family collection Saturdays could be viewed as a harvest of sorts as well. While crops were seasonal, the other businesses provided weekly gains usually.

On Saturdays, Granny and Grandpa would ride from house to house and town to town to collect what was owed in payments for a house that had been built or for rent. They would collect the payments and Granny would write a receipt for the money received. A friend of mine some years later fondly recalled that his parent's first home was located in LaFrance, South Carolina, and built by the Head family. They paid a little over one dollar a week on it. They would put the money in a little envelope and both Grandpa and Granny came together every Saturday to collect the weekly payment. Most of the kids were involved in riding around from time to time for the collections to be made. They spoke of fond memories such as the smell of cottonseed meal made at the Roller Mill in LaFrance/Pendleton area. They said the aroma was nice to smell as they rode by. They met and interacted with lots of nice people over the years.

Doris recalled that collecting money was sometimes entertaining. One time when they approached a house to collect a payment, the small kids came to the door and said their momma said to tell them she wasn't there. Granny grinned and told the kids to tell their momma, who was hiding under the house where Granny could see her, to cover her legs next time. On another occasion, a man saw them coming and lay down in a ditch to hide from them. When they saw him, they asked what he was doing, he replied, "My teethies are hurting me really bad!!" If a payment couldn't be made, for whatever reason, they would just try again the following week to collect. Another fond memory that Doris recalled involved John. Before going out to collect one Saturday, Granny had cooked a big pot of pumpkin and left it on the stove to cool. Doris went with Grandpa and Granny that day to collect while the boys were left home. While they were gone, a big storm came up. When Granny got home and found the boys to be fine, she asked John what he thought about the storm. He replied, "I thought you could have at least left some bread to go with the punkin." Granny just laughed. Obviously the storm was no match against a hungry stomach.

As stated earlier, several times the generosity of my grandfather and grandmother was witnessed on these collection Saturdays as folks needed help. Late payments, no payments, giving food, and other generosities when needed were often on display. Sowing seeds of kindness and forgiveness was Biblical and a harvest of unknown proportions awaited them as their Heavenly reward.

Chapter Nine

GROWING UP

LOTS OF MEMORIES remain related to the kids just growing up and being kids. Hunting and fishing was always a big past time and often came with rewards. James and Lee Hawkins used to kill birds using a sling shot. Apparently James was an expert marksman with a sling shot. He killed pigeons and even a blue heron. James made slingshots out of the rubber lining from a tire. He and Lee also built a small building that they would stay in at times. It had heat and they cooked in it. James and the boys liked building campfires and roasting potatoes. Often birds and other wildlife would be cooked over a campfire as well if their hunting had been successful. According to John, ketchup was the condiment of choice, especially used to cover the reddened parts of the meat that didn't cook quite enough over an open fire. "That worked ok for rabbits and squirrels but not so well for opossum," he said. It needed to be cooked all the way through!!!

The boys would go seining at a creek and catch "red horse" fish. Charles said they looked sort of like gold fish. They were very small. They would catch hundreds at a time and then fry them up. They would make a sein out of a two hundred pound size fertilizer bags. For one person, they would place 2 sticks across it and for two people; they would rip the bag down the middle to make it larger and then put a stick on each side. Now that's ingenuity! They would usually go to Oliver's Lake, which was around Twelve Mile Lake today in Clemson. They also had several swimming holes, where at times a little skinny dipping may have taken place. Kelly Mill pond, Cox pond and Cateechee River or Beach, as it was sometimes called, were places they frequented. John recalls learning to swim in Cox Pond. It was located close to Aunt Berline's home in Central. Cateechee River had a dam and was near the mill in Cateechee. They also recalled how sometimes their legs would be covered with leeches when they came out of Oliver's Lake. I also recall my dad referring to leeches covering his legs after being in some of the lakes growing up.

Other activities included playing tag in the cow pastures, climbing trees, playing kick the can, horseshoes and other games. They had a few toys, but mainly made their own. They would take an old car tire and roll it along and play police. They made play money out of cola and milk caps. John said they finally got a bike in their teens. He and my mom, Annie, would take turns riding it in the evenings and even after dark. John recalls meeting my dad, Harold Rowland, for the first time, when he and a friend came down to Head Town and played horseshoes with them. That is where my dad met my mom, Annie.

On weekends, the boys played ball in Central, Midway, Norris or Cateechee. Their team usually won when they had 3 "professional" ball players on their team. One was a pitcher, a hind catcher and an infielder. These 3 had come to town and rented a house nearby while they laid tile for various places. When they weren't busy, my uncles and others recruited them to play with the Central team. They pretty much won every game when they were playing, including beating the Midway team that was always pretty good. The term professional is used loosely here. They had played organized baseball of sorts, but whether it was college or league play my uncles do not recall. The Head boys mainly played in the outfield. John remembers often the Cateechee players walking to Central and then playing the game. My dad also played with my uncles and pitched. He was a right handed pitcher. My dad told my brothers of one game in which he pitched a no hitter for 18 innings only for his team to lose one to nothing. John recalls that the mill league games were big and taken serious in the area. All of the local mills had ball teams. Games would be played on Saturdays and usually they had a big attendance as there wasn't much else to bid for their attention. Mills in the area included Central, Norris, LaFrance and one in Williamston that had teams. Locations were rotated for each game.

The boys also had part time jobs outside of the family while growing up to make them a little extra money. On weekends, Charles would plow garden spots for some of the folks in Central. John had a newspaper route covering half of Central and the mill village. He drove the Model A car and his dog, named Brown, followed him on the route. At some point John began to notice that more dogs followed him in addition to Brown. Five or so dogs turned into ten or so and finally up to twenty or thirty dogs followed him while driving the route. The paper was delivered around 4 am so the dogs barking disturbed some folks and some of the dogs messed with flower beds and such on the route. John finally quite because of all of the commotion involved with the dogs. He had the route for a year.

Paul was known to be a prankster. After Annie and Harold (my mom and dad) got married, they lived down below Grandpa and Granny. My dad worked the evening shift at Cannon Mills, leaving Mom alone at home. There was a little dirt hill outside one of the windows of their house. Paul decided to trick my mom. He covered himself in a sheet and stood outside the window on the hill. My mom saw it and became scared. She later told Paul about what she saw and he pretended to help her search for the ghost. The ghost appeared on several occasions until one day someone found Paul's hiding place for the sheet he had used to cover himself.

Driving and learning to drive was a past time as well as a necessity. John recalls they had a Model A car and Granny taught him to drive. Granny would drive to Seneca to get corn and John would always drive back. He said during those days that roads were dirt, and a trip to Greenville would take all day to drive there and back from Central. Cars could register around 60 mph, but 30 mph was fast. John remembers driving the log truck to court Clara Bryant, whom he married in 1950.

John also recalled a time when he and Annie went with their parents to visit Lola at college in Cullowhee, North Carolina, around Christmas time. Grandpa drove the Model A car. John recalled that every few miles they would have to stop and fill it with water to prevent it from overheating. They stopped at restaurants, gas stations, or even creeks to get water. They went to Seneca and then through Highlands before they crossed over to get to their destination. That seemed out of the way, but those were the roads available at the time. He also recalled it was very cold and he and Annie kept warm by having a lantern in the backseat that gave off some heat. The car did not have a heater. After the Model A car, the next family car they would own was a 1934 Ford. John remembered later on when Grandpa bought a new truck in 1947. It cost $1,300. The next year, Grandpa bought another new truck for business. The 1948 model price was $1,500. They were amazed at such a price increase in a year! John's first car was a used one that cost around $100. John also recalled that after my mom and dad got married, he and Charles taught them both how to drive. Once they got the hang of it, they would take road trips to Rosman to visit family and practice driving. Mom and dad's first car was a 1939 Mercury.

John also recalled a time several of the kids and grandkids went to the apple orchard. They ate apples and drank apple cider. On the way back, John was driving. In those days, kids stood up if they wanted to in the car. There were no seat belts. One of the kids stood in the back seat behind John and as he drove them home, got sick and threw up on his neck and down his back. He laughed as he told that story, even though it was not funny at the time. One time, John and Clara, along with Doris and another family member took a day trip that wound up in Kentucky. They came across a place with caves and cave tours being offered. They went to tour the cave, but Clara stayed in the car as she was pregnant. There was a gallon of water in the car, and she drank most of it while waiting for them to return. On the way home, John was ready to get home and didn't want to make many stops. Clara let it be known that stops were needed as she had drunk a gallon of water, and it was a long ride home. Stops were made as needed.

Granny and Grandpa often took Sunday rides to Crow Creek in the Salem area, and some of the kids, would go as well. It seemed that no matter where they planned to go, they always wound up going the same route and ending up in Crow Creek. Granny made plates of food for everyone going. They would leave after church was over and be so hungry that they started eating on the way up. Granny would start eating hers as well and Grandpa, while driving, would reach over and grab something off of Granny's plate. She would tell him that was her plate and he had his own!!! He would finally pull over somewhere to stop and they would all finish eating. There were no paper plates and plastic utensils, so real plates and silverware were used and taken back home to wash and use again.

Doris fondly recalled how Lois always took care of her and let her tag along for various things. Lois was around 20 years old when Doris was born, so she often watched Doris when Granny was busy in the store and such. Lois took writing and cooking classes in town. She would let Doris come along with her. Doris always loved to go because they had snacks in the class and she got one as well. She thinks it was a fruit flavored drink and a small sandwich, but she always looked forward to going with Lois. On another occasion, she went with Lois by bus to the town of Liberty to a department store around Easter. When they went into the store, Doris saw a huge Easter basket and had to have it!! Lois told her that it was too big and too expensive. Doris said she kept on pleading for the basket and Lois finally bought it for her. They could barely fit it on the bus to make it home because it was so big. They did make it back home and Doris said she has the best Easter basket around for that Easter! She was proud of it. Doris also remembered that Lois took her to school for the first time. Lois told Doris to stay in a specific area until her name was called. Lois left and went back home. After a long period of time, Doris decided they were not going to call her name so she left and went back home and went out to the store. When Granny saw her, she asked what she was doing there and Doris told her they didn't call her name. Granny walked her back to school.

Doris also remembered when Harold and Lola married that she wanted to move in with them. She packed a dress and her small rocking chair to take to their house. She stayed with them as much as she could. Harold and Lola worked at Cannon Mills on the second shift. Doris remembers many visits with them after they got off of work. Doris was known to play a prank or two during those visits on Harold. Doris would later meet her love, Roger Riggins, at a birthday party. They started dating afterwards and were later married.

Chapter Ten

ON THE FARM

FARMING WAS A way of life and part of the livelihood for the Head family, as well as for many others in the area. They planted large wheat and cornfields for harvest and then took it to the Roller Mill in Central where It was made into flour and cornmeal that the family used and also could be sold in the store. They grew their own vegetables as well. The produce was picked, prepared and taken to the cannery in Central, not far from their home, where the vegetables would be canned and preserved.

In order to grow the crops, a lot of plowing had to be done throughout the farming season. Charles was taught to drive a tractor around the age of twelve by a fellow called Big Boy. He taught him how to plow fields. During the peak of the season, Charles would leave home around 7 am on the tractor and drive to the farm place and plow until noon. He would come back home for lunch, fill the tractor up with gas and then return to the fields and plow until 6pm. That schedule later would change a little as Grandpa would bring the gas and a brown bag lunch to Charles at the farm around noon each day. In 1952 and 1953 they got new tractors. The new tractor had lights, so Charles plowed at night as well, when needed. The 1953 tractor was the Jubilee model.

In addition to automobiles, "Henry Ford was interested in farming machinery. He grew up in a family of farmers outside of Detroit, when the work was extremely hard and nothing got done without hard labor. As his interest in automobiles grew, he also expressed a desire to 'lift the burden of farming from flesh and blood and place it on steel and motors.' In 1953, Ford released a Golden Jubilee model tractor as part of the 50th anniversary celebration of Ford. The first experimental Ford tractor was built in 1907, called an "Automobile Plow" and was introduced to American farmers in 1918. Ford called his first, mass-produced tractor the Fordson and it created an affordable piece of machinery to farmers, and made it possible for the average farmer to purchase a new and reliable tractor. The Fordson tractor was the first lightweight, mass produced tractor on the market and the name of the tractor was a take on the original name of the tractor operation, Henry Ford & Son."[44]

In addition to gardening, there were others chores to be done as well. Annie used to milk the cows. When Charles was around twelve, Granny told him she would give him 15 cents if he let Annie teach him how to milk the cows. He earned the money, and later on his job became milking the cows routinely. Cows were milked and any extra milk not used for cooking and drinking was made into butter. Granny would put milk in the churn and cream would rise to the top. When it clabbered, it would produce butter and they would place the butter in a wooden mold that had a flower design on it. The molds made pound or half pound sizes. The flower emblem would appear on the pat of butter when removed from the mold. They would feed the cows beet pulp and cottonseed meal to get them to produce more milk.

They also raised hogs. Weather had to be just right before one could be killed. They would listen to the weather report on the radio. It had to be cold for 3 days, but couldn't be freezing. Friends, Jim and Harry, killed the hogs for them and all would be involved in processing the meat. All parts of the hog were processed. Souse meat was meat taken from around the brain. It was gelled or molded together and then sliced to cook and eat. Another dish was made using pork brains and mixing with scrambled eggs. Liver mush was made by mixing liver with a little corn meal to thicken it and make it sliceable. Fat back or bacon was often served. Sausage would be made by mixing several portions of the meat together and seasoning with hot pepper and sage. Then sausage could be fried up into patties. Fat could be rendered and cracklings made. Intestines cleaned and bleached for chitterlings. The kids stated that Granny cooked wonderful chitterlings. She cleaned them and boiled them for a long time. She then battered in buttermilk and flour and fried them. Crackling corn bread was a favorite as well.

Chickens were also raised. When one was needed for dinner, they would go outside and select one, kill it and prepare for cooking. Chicken and eggs were plentiful. All of the chicken was processed as well. Liver and gizzards were common part of the chicken eaten in those days. Chicken had no teeth, so digestion basically occurred in the gizzard. The gizzard is part of the digestive tract that grinds everything the bird eats. While processing the chicken, the gizzard was split open and cleaned of any gritty remains. Then, it would be boiled and then fried. [45] Pully bones were also salvaged. They were also known as the wishbone. Part of the breast plate of the chicken, the V shape thin bone would be held by 2 people and they would pull on it until it broke. The person holding the largest piece of the bone would be the recipient of good luck. Because the hens laid eggs, the task was to kill a rooster for dinner and leave the hens. One time one of the younger boys wanted to kill the chicken for the meal with his BB gun. He went outside and wound up killing a hen. The kids, being kids, said to him: "Amen brother Ben, shot a rooster but killed a hen."

Even with a large family, usually just one chicken was cooked for a meal and each person had a designated piece of chicken they would get to eat. Grandpa got the breast and Granny got the back. Other pieces were distributed by age and so on, but each knew what their piece would be at meal time. If any of the kids wanted the heart or kidneys, they had to call for it before cooking it. Nothing was wasted in those days. Because of the necessity of just killing one chicken for a meal and keeping the others for laying eggs, the development of popular chicken recipes probably came into play. Chicken and dumplings was one recipe that could extend a chicken for large amounts. Dumplings made from flour and milk cooked in a pot of cooked chicken went a long way in filling up a crew of kids. Chicken pot pie with a flour crust covering chicken and vegetables could extend the meal as well.

Also on some of Grandpa's property were numerous wild blackberry bushes. They picked large tins full of them. They were used in making cobblers, jams, and jellies. As we grew up, my brother Tom and I would pick gallons of blackberries in the summer in the pastures near our house and sell them to a neighbor for a few dollars. We found ways to make money. Along with getting blackberries, we got chiggers as well. Chiggers were small mites that clung to plants and shrubs in the forest. If you walked by the bushes and knocked them onto you, they would bite. You may not know it at that very moment, but later on there would be redness, swelling, itching and whelps around the area. There were many tales centered on how to heal the bite. Peroxide, rubbing alcohol, bleach and nail polish were all remedies rumored to help. Basically it took a lot of time and refrain from scratching for healing to occur. Poison oak was another irritant. Working or playing outdoors often led to small clustered whelps that were red, swollen and itchy as well. Many tales centered around treatment for poison oak also. From those for chigger bites to calamine lotion and other creams, numerous remedies were employed for treatment. Allergic reactions to the poison oak often required shots of steroid from the doctor to relieve the discomfort and promote healing.

Many of the farming practices and traditions became a mainstay for future generations as the kids and their families continued to farm even after they married and left home. My mom and dad farmed pretty much their entire life. Gardening began in the spring, especially on Good Friday before Easter, or at other times when the *Farmer's Almanac* revealed best times for planting. These times were related to the phases of the moon and weather predictions. Sometimes they also used what is today referred to as the zodiac man of signs, where body parts were associated with signs and dates and you only planted certain vegetables when the signs were in specific body parts for optimal production. It was hard to argue with these methods as they grew enough vegetables to feed their kids, the neighbors and many others as well. That was in addition to my mom preserving and canning food every summer. While many kids discussed their travel plans over the summer and different events, my family had one summer event. Gardening and canning. While we kids vehemently disliked it at the time, today nothing tastes better than fresh grown vegetables or those canned by your own hands for use later on. It was farm to table before that was fashionable. Even today, some of my cousins and I get together with my aunt Doris to make jellies and jams and other items to can and preserve. Those days are always fun and special. Using signs from the Almanac was important for other entities along with gardening. Before pulling a tooth or performing other procedures at home or visiting a doctor, the calendar would be consulted. This was also important when mothers who were breast feeding their babies were planning to wean them. The signs had to be right for success. The information on the moon phases, zodiac man signs and such were found every year from a calendar that came from the Central Roller Mill and later on Pendleton Oil Mill. These calendars were given at the end of each year to their patrons. My mom and dad had to have one of those calendars every year for planning purposes. It could sort of be described as the gardening bible for farmers.

Another astrological entity was dog days of summer. This timeframe from July to September welcomed hot muggy summer weather to the south. For some, it represented a time to slow down and maybe head to the mountains, sit back in the shade with sweet tea or RC Cola, go to the creek or whatever you could do to stay cool. This phenomenon takes its name from the Dog Star in the constellation Canis Major, the brightest star in the sky that would rise and set with the sun. [46]Folks believed this to be the cause for the extended hot and muggy weather. One tale that always was told was that snakes would go blind during this time frame, so there was a need to be extra careful around them, as if an excuse was needed.

Most of the Head family had a dislike and fear of snakes. This was a family gene passed down to many, including myself and my siblings. My mom was known for her fear of snakes. In the garden during the summer months, it would not be uncommon to come across a snake. My dad was usually at work, so if she saw one, a loud scream of "snaaaake" could be heard by the neighbors above and below on either side of our house. The houses were not a few feet away, mind you. When they heard, they came running and the first to arrive would kill the snake for my mom. My mom shared one story of how one day she was picking okra and had a basket full. She looked down and saw a snake. She threw the basket down, started screaming and ran off. She said the snake could have that okra. A funny tale related to dead snakes was to hang the dead creature over a fence and it would rain within three days. When one was killed, over the fence it would go because rain was welcomed during the summer for gardens, cooling off and such. Someone would always say to not kill non-poisonous snakes as they were good for the environment. My mom would look anyone in the eye and say any snake was poisonous. She never met a non-poisonous snake that I know of.

Getting back to weather, blackberry winter was another phenomenon as well. The transition from winter to summer would have some periods of cold weather intermingled within it. A cold spell during May occurred when blackberry bushes were in bloom giving rise to the name blackberry winter in the South. There were many other weather tales in the south as well. If it was raining and the sun came out, it was going to be raining the same time the next day. Another tale said if the sun was shining as it rained that the devil was beating his wife. If there was a ring or haze around the moon, it would rain in three days. If it thundered in the wintertime, there would be snow on the ground within a week. If there were foggy mornings in the month of August, the number of those mornings represented the number of snows that would fall in the coming winter. My mom had Christmas and Thanksgiving cactus plants and they only bloomed around those holidays. She also had rain flower potted plants. If any of them bloomed during the summer, it would rain within three days of a budding or bloom. If caterpillars or wooly worms were extra fuzzy in the fall that symbolized a harsh winter was ahead. If the corn shucks on ears of corn were extra thick that harvest or if there were a lot of acorns on the ground in the fall, it would be a harsh winter. If you heard a tree frog, there would be rain within three days. As strange as these tales may seem, there is a holiday in February taunting the weather skills of a ground hog.

Buckeye trees were popular and plentiful back in the day. They did not predict the weather in any way that I know of, but the seed/nut that fell from them was called a buckeye and it was said to bring good luck. Lots of men would carry a buckeye around in their pocket or women would sometimes carry them in their purse. As long as I can remember, my dad carried one in the front pocket of his pants. He carried a small pocket knife as well. Back in the day, I think it was a rite of manhood in the South to carry a pocket knife. Anyway, when my dad passed away, he still had a couple of small buckeyes and pocket knife that he kept close by. Today, when most people hear the word buckeye, they probably think of a chocolate peanut butter confection or of a college football team with that nickname. I, on the other hand, think of my dad.

Chapter Eleven

FOOD AND FIXINGS

BACK IN THE day, counting calories or watching fat intake or cholesterol count were not issues. Most people were happy to get the food to eat and certainly not worried about their waist line. It was certainly fresh and one didn't have to worry about what additives and such were mixed in. Whether gains came from hunting or fishing or raising your own, food and preparing it was important. From daily harvesting and cooking to traditions passed down, food of all types was important. Families ate their meals together which allowed for time to interact with each other. Grace was said before each meal to give thanks for the food and to acknowledge God's goodness. On Sundays the table would especially be filled with lots of delicious food and the Head family was no exception. Often, a pastor would be invited to come to their house and eat lunch. The smaller kids didn't always like this as they would have to wait until the guests had finished eating before they could eat. Granny would run ahead and get in the kitchen to make sure everything looked good and everything was properly prepared as company was sometimes a surprise. One story is told of Lola not looking forward to company for one Sunday dinner. A Rev. Hawkins was preaching at their church and had been invited to join them afterwards. Probably tired of doing the cooking for the day and already hungry, in conversation she said to someone, "Why are we inviting reverse Hawkins to dinner today?" She obviously had a different interpretation for the Rev abbreviation for reverend. The irony in this story is that later on she would marry the reverend's son, Harold Hawkins.

Over time, the methods for cooking changed with the arrival of modern appliances and cookware, but what was cooked may or may not have changed. From roasting game over the campfire as described by John and Charles, to catching, cleaning, and freezing game after a successful hunt, cooking game was one time popular. Granny grew up in the mountains learning how to cook game, but Grandpa didn't eat any varmints of any kind as he would call them. According to Doris, Grandpa didn't like shrimp and even referred to them as varmints as well. He told Granny one time to throw the pan away as Edna had cooked "shwimps" in it. Even though they were not necessarily fond of shrimp, they did love oysters. Gallons of oysters would sometimes arrive along with the boxes of fish, which Grandpa ordered and were delivered by train. They were a big hit with the kids and sometimes the oysters as well as a few of the fish didn't make it to the fish fries. John fondly recalled as they would open the boxes of fish, and with ice still covering them, he would sometimes grab one and run cook and eat it before anyone knew he had done it. They always looked forward to the fish and oysters arriving. Oyster stew and fried oysters were a hit among the kids for sure, along with fried fish.

Varmints and critters aside, lots of good food was prepared and the techniques for cooking and the recipes used were passed down as well. Boiling and frying were common methods unless an out-side fire was used for roasting. Cast iron skillets were a main staple in cookware. Cornbread could be made in a round cast iron skillet and the corn bread cut into wedge slices after it was done and ready to be served. It could also be made in stick like shapes and be called a pone, or shaped like pancakes and called hoecakes or made into muffins. It could also be made into balls and deep fried to make hush puppies that was served at a fish fry or cookout. And of course, cornbread is the base in the south for dressing served with the turkey at Thanksgiving. Cornbread went with everything but especially a mess of greens or beans. It was used to sop up the pot liquor left from greens. Pot liquor was the juice or liquid left behind when greens were cooked and served. After meals were finished, any leftover cornbread would be eaten later crumbled up in a glass of milk or buttermilk, and eaten with a spoon. Cornbread or biscuits were staples. Biscuits were served with molasses and butter over them. Jellies and jams and butter sandwiched in between two halves of a biscuit went over well. Gravy smothering biscuits is another southern tradition. Milk and water were added to the skillet after cooking any type of meat to mix with the meat droppings and then was thickened with a little flour. Gravy would then be served over the meat, vegetables such as mashed potatoes or the biscuit. Gravy was one way to make a meal go farther in a big household, while making the meal tasty as well. Red eye gravy could be made when coffee replaced the water or milk in the process and served with country ham and grits. Grits were a food group in itself. Cooked with milk or just water, butter and salt were a must. Cheese also was a favorite ingredient to add to grits. They could be served at breakfast or at supper. My mom cooked lots of grits for the grandkids to eat when they visited and spent the night. A large pot of grits would be needed to fill up hungry kids. Grits would be served with toast and homemade jelly or her famous apple butter. Another tradition in the Rowland household and some others as well, was placing a slice of tomato in the biscuit, sort of a tomato sandwich using a biscuit as the bread. My husband, Clint, had never heard of this oddity when we first met. He later decided this was a "Central" thing to do. He was from Anderson, South Carolina, where they obviously did not know about good stuff or "fine eating" as my mom would say. However, tomato sandwiches were and continue to be a staple in the South, using Dukes brand mayonnaise spread over white bread and then slices of tomato placed on one side of the bread. You could go a little crazy or wild and add a slice of cheese, bologna, ham or other meat to it. In addition to tomato sandwiches, pimento cheese sandwiches were a staple. Pimento cheese had many recipes, but all included a variety of cheese, mayonnaise and pimentos or roasted peppers.

Southern cooking and eating cannot be discussed without talking about sweet tea to wash it down. Ice cold tea and a hot sweltering day in the South go hand in hand. Initially, tea was served with alcoholic beverages in fancy crystal glasses, but, after prohibition, tea remained as a refreshing beverage to continue to use the fancy glass ware. [47] With refrigeration, tea went from a rare treat to a staple at the dinner table as well.

Lots of food was prepared over time with some dishes standing out above others. Grandpa in his later years made chicken and dumplings for almost every meal when he had to cook for himself. Granny made her version of mashed potatoes, but called them "mashed down taters". Potatoes could also be sliced and fried or cubed, boiled or made into potato salad. Originating in Germany, potato salad became a southern dish when adding mayonnaise and serving it cold. Cole slaw was a Dutch dish meaning cold cabbage and deviled eggs originated in Italy. All three were given a southern twist and were served at special meals. Whether for Sunday or potluck dinners or Holiday meals, this trio was usually around. A very simple dessert was the pear salad. Grated cheese mixed with mayonnaise and placed in a halved pear that usually came from a can. A maraschino cherry was placed on top and the pears were usually placed on top of lettuces leaves that covered a plate for decoration. While cobblers originated in Europe being filled with meat and covered with a crust, southerners made cobblers using a flour mixture and fresh fruit of the season. Originating outside of the United States, pound cake recipes initially called for a pound each of flour, sugar, eggs and butter. Over time the quantities of each ingredient were decreased and additional flavors added to make the pound cake a southern culinary fixture.

Macaroni and cheese was also a staple in any southern feast. However, macaroni and tomatoes were my comfort food and still remain so today. My mom would open a quart jar of her canned tomatoes and place in the pot. She put in a small box of elbow macaroni, butter and salt and cooked it until the macaroni became tender. If she knew I was running by the house for a minute in the later years, she would have a bowl made for me. I could eat some there and take the rest with me. That is one of my most treasured memories. For many years, I tried duplicating the recipe exactly, but it never tasted like hers. In later years as I have on some occasions been able to make the dish taste almost like my mom made it, I have defined those moments as a true measure of success in my culinary skills.

While southern food was very flavorful, any discussion centered on food was a language of its own. Once someone had eaten all that they possibly could, they could be heard saying either "I am as full as a tick or I am going to pop." Either way, it was a compliment to the cook. If there were beans or greens to cook, or any other food item for that matter, the amount wasn't measured by weight. It was always a mess of beans or mess of greens. A mess meant enough of the item to feed a family of 2 or 6 or 10. You had enough. Greens could consist of collard greens alone or a mixture of turnip greens, mustard greens, kale, spinach and any other leafy green. Turnip greens were the only green in the group mentioned to have a root vegetable attached to it, the turnip. Another popular green in the spring was poke salad (pronounced poke sallat.) It was a wild green that grew in the woods or even alongside some roads. The leaves could be cooked, but you had to be careful when cooking them. The smaller and younger stalks were the ones picked as poisonous berries grew on the stalk as it aged. Thus, all of the leaves were cleaned vigorously and cooked twice. My parents always said that one mess of poke sallat in the spring cured whatever ailed you.

Significant expressions centered on food and cooking were very common. The pot calling the kettle black was said if someone was guilty of doing the same thing they were complaining about someone else doing. You couldn't get blood out of a turnip was said if you couldn't routinely get someone to do something you asked of them. Sour grapes indicated a bad feeling about something after it was done. If someone was nice to look at, they were pretty as a peach. Give me some sugar wasn't asking about the sweet stuff. That was asking for a kiss. If you loved someone a bushel and a peck, you loved them a lot. If someone was slow to get around and get things done, they were slow as molasses. If something wasn't important, it didn't amount to a hill of beans. Whole milk was sweet milk, as opposed to buttermilk. There weren't any one or two percent options. You also didn't cry over spilled milk. This meant to move forward after something happened that you wish hadn't. Having a RC cola and moon pie or dropping peanuts in your cola bottle before drinking it were two southern traditions when snacking.

Canning or freezing was referred to as putting up. Putting up four quarts of green beans meant four quarts were canned or possibly frozen. Even though roasting is a cooking term, in the south it was a description for being hot. Someone might say, It was so hot that I was about to roast.

Chapter Twelve

ANIMAL LORE

ONE CAN IMAGINE with all of the livestock around, some of the animals became pets. They would receive special attention at least for a while. According to Charles and John, James had a Billy goat that he would hook up to a small wagon and be pulled around in. His name was Billy. They recalled seeing a goat for sale one day while working in Pendleton. They bought it for a dollar or so and brought it back home for James. John had a pet pig that followed him around and even slept with him. He was called Pig. Doris had a pet pig as well. He fell in a ditch and got hurt and died. They had a cow named Ludy. Raymond, one of the workers, named her. Doris recalled that if you had a cowlick in your hair, it was called a Ludy Lick.

Several pets claimed special attention from the family. There would be several dogs over the years that were remembered. One was named Boy. Granny had two small dogs that she named Peatrice and Tilly. Douglas, aka Doogie, might be the most memorable pet of the family. He would be the last pet they had. Doogie was a very smart dog. He rode in the front seat with Grandpa, often in his lap, as they would take their evening ride. Sometimes from a distance, it looked as if Doogie was driving the car. He was fed table food, especially fried chicken and chicken and dumplings. He had an electric blanket to keep him warm during the winters. If he didn't appear to be feeling well, Grandpa would give him a Dristan (over the counter medicine) to help perk him up. Granny told of a story one morning around 3 am she woke up and Grandpa was not in the bed. She got up to go check on him. She found Grandpa and he told her that he had just gotten back. Doogie wasn't feeling well and he took him for a ride in the car to get some fresh air.

One tale is told of a grandson who took Grandpa to a flea market in Pickens. When he picked Grandpa up and initially saw that Doogie was going as well, he was a little worried. He just knew Doogie would get out and get lost. Anyway, after they arrived and got out of the car to start walking through the area, Doogie walked right beside Grandpa. After Grandpa went a short distance, he bought a bag of goodies and gave the bag to Doogie. Doogie then carried the bag in his mouth. As Grandpa would stop to look at things, Doogie would drop the bag and proceed to snack on a treat from the bag until Grandpa was ready to walk forward. Doogie would then pick the bag up and keep walking alongside Grandpa. After a while the grandson and Grandpa split up to look at different things and agreed to meet back at the car at 11 am. The grandson got there a couple minutes before 11. He looked and Doogie came walking to the car right at 11. Grandpa came shortly after.

On another occasion, Grandpa and some others were in the town of Easley and stopped to get gas in the car. Doogie got out and walked around. After pumping the gas, they went into the store. When they got into the car to return home, they forgot about Doogie. They were a few miles down the road before Grandpa realized they didn't have Doogie. They turned the car around and headed back to the gas station. When they arrived, Doogie was patiently sitting at the edge of the road, waiting for them to come back and get him. Grandpa would often be in the kitchen making dumplings or going to the store to get fried chicken after Granny died. When asked what he was doing, he just replied, "Well, Doogie's got to eat."

The Rowland family did not suffer any shortage on dogs. However, most of them were hunting dogs that my dad would raise and train in their area of expertise. There were bird dogs, coon hounds and beagles. There would be hundreds of them in total over the years. A few of them hung around for a long time and made the hall of fame so to speak among the family. Trouble and Lady were bird dogs and hunted quail. Blue was a blue tick coon hound and Mac was a red tick hound dog. They hunted squirrels, opossum and raccoons. Beagles were the rabbit hunters. We did have a beagle pup named Fiesty, who became more of a pet than a hunter. We had several cats over the years as well. They were supposed to help keep snakes away, so obviously my mom would say" the more the merrier," but my dad would have a say as well. The first cat that I had that I recall was a calico named Bess. We had a large grey tom cat named Charlie that let every other cat in the area know who was boss. We had lots of others that were named after baseball players and so on over the years. My current cats were born around the home place in Central, making them extra special to me.

I have often marveled at our southern language and the influence of animals. Using animal behavior and characteristics to describe a situation or behavior in humans is a practice still used today. The following are just some of the numerous southern sayings centering on animals. Grinning like a possum. If you have ever seen a possum or a picture of one up close, they do appear to be wearing a smile. If something hadn't occurred in a long time, it was a coon's age length of time. For example, he was grinning like a possum because he hadn't seen his honey in a coon's age as she returned home. Grinning is not to be confused with playing possum. Playing possum was another way of saying someone was faking something. A person could be stubborn as an old mule. If a mule didn't want to work or do what you wanted, it took a lot of convincing to get it headed in the right direction. The same was true for some folks. If you took the bull by the horns, you needed to approach or confront someone and get something straightened out. If a person was feeling real good about himself, or maybe a little too confident, someone would try to bring him back to reality, so to speak, and tell him to get off his high horse. If a person was getting carried away with something too fast, he would be told to hold your horses. If someone really got to you, he got your goat. If you stayed out too late, someone would say in the morning that you were out until the cows came home. Strong as an ox would be a compliment to someone's strength.

If you were going down a pig trail or rabbit hole, it meant you were distracted or gotten off of the subject. If you cut yourself and the bleeding was hard to stop, you were bleeding like a stuck pig. If there was a good harvest, you would be eating high off the hog. That was not to be confused with putting on the dog, which is what one did if they really went out of their way to impress someone.

If someone was really sick, he was sick as a dog. If a person hung out a lot or spent a lot of time with another person, he was like a tic on a dog. Barking up the wrong tree was not good. Neither was raining cats and dogs. If you ever tried to gets lots of things done at one time or a lot of people on the same page, it was similar to herding cats. If someone had stayed away for a long time before returning, you would hear upon his arrival, look what the cat dragged in. If you couldn't keep a secret and spoiled the surprise, you let the cat of the bag.

If you were expecting something to happen or making big plans, you might be told to don't count your chickens before they hatch. This meant that things may not always happen the way you anticipate. Speaking of chickens, if something was scarce as hen's teeth, it was pretty rare because chickens don't have teeth. Blind as a bat indicated you couldn't see well. Knee high to a grasshopper referred to being of a very young age.

Mad as a hornet. If you ever disturbed a hornet or wasp nest, you know what this means. Wet hens didn't have a good reputation, either. "Madder than a wet hen" was being pretty upset as well. Having a bee in your bonnet wasn't much better but being busy as a bee could be a good thing. If you had been looking for something and just overlooked it, someone would say, "It was right there. If it had been a snake it would have bitten you." If someone was really lazy and didn't work, they were so lazy they wouldn't hit a lick at a snake. If someone was very poor, they were as poor as a field mouse. If someone tried to store something or hide it away, this was referred to as squirreling something away. They squirreled their extra pennies away for a rainy day. You could also make a mountain out of a mole hill if you worried about something or talked about it too much. The straw that broke the camel's back was not good. This meant that things had piled up and finally one last thing added was enough to break the load. If a black cat ran out in front of you while driving, you would have bad luck. If a red bird appeared in your yard, you would have company. If the cows were lying down in the pasture, the fish were biting.

Wives tales and sayings were a big part of daily conversation in the south as well. Wives tales are not as popular today, but some of those sayings still are for sure. Sometimes the tales and reality collided. Lots of wives tales centered on health. If someone was having hiccups, you did something to scare them to make the hiccups stop. For example, yelling "snake" was always popular in my household to scare someone. If someone started choking as they drank something, my mom always said to bend their ear over and they would stop coughing. If you were outside in the rain or snow in the winter and your head got wet, you would get sick in just a day or two. That was my mom's favorite. If you read in a dark room, you would go blind. If you sat too close to the television while watching it, your eyesight would go bad.

After a baby was born, the navel cord was a little scab over the umbilical cord and would usually fall off in about one to two weeks. My mom always told my sisters-in-law and others to burn the navel cord in a little fire. This would prevent the child from bed wetting later on when they became toilet trained. I have to say that I think that somewhat worked for my nieces and nephews. There were several tales about how to determine the sex of a baby before birth as well. How the mother carried the baby in her stomach, either high or low would determine the sex. If a ring placed on a string and held over the mother's stomach moved in a certain direction it predicted the sex.

A lot of the other sayings centered on how to treat people. Before judging someone in how they reacted or responded to something, you needed to walk a mile in their shoes. If doing this, your perspective would surely change. The shoe is on the other foot now is sort of similar as well. You think about things one way, but then it changes and you have to rethink it. As children we were never to get too big for our britches, meaning never think you are better than others. My mom always told us kids that one day we would look back and ask where did the time go? She said as children, "all you want to do is turn eighteen so that you can become an adult. You never think you are going to get there, but you climb the hill until you do, and then it is downhill from there ". My parents often said that there was not anything good on the streets at night after 11 pm. Guess what time curfew was? If you were looking for something hard to find, it was like looking for a needle in a haystack.

There was a lot of wisdom in some of the wives tales and sayings. All were developed from observation and deep thought when you really get down to it. Knowing what they witnessed or knew about things at the time, opinions were developed. Those simple sayings involved common foods, animals, weather observations and people. If we follow some of those recommendations today, or put the same effort into thinking things through, just think of the landmarks we could develop or solidify.

Chapter Thirteen

CHALLENGING TIMES

IN ADDITION TO the humble beginnings of ambulances, medical care was very different from today. Before telephones, someone had to go to get the doctor and then the doctor traveled to the home to see the patient in an emergency. They made house calls. Nurse midwives came to homes to help deliver babies or to check on the mother after delivery. Minimal medications and equipment limited diagnosis of ailments and treatment of injuries and conditions.

Hospitals throughout the upstate were named or added Memorial Hospital to their name in order to honor those service personnel who fought and died for our country. Most of these hospitals in the area provided general care. Shriners Hospital for Children was an exception. "Opened in 1927, in Greenville, South Carolina, Shriners Hospital served the needs of children with orthopaedic or neuromuscular needs. This was made possible by a large donation of money from Greenville business men to start the hospital. Today, Shriners remains one of 22 hospitals in an international health care system providing pediatric specialty care for a wide range of orthopaedic and neuromuscular conditions."[48] Shriners became a pivotal part of three of the Head children during their youths. The Head family would learn a lot about Shriners Hospital. John stayed at Shriners Children Hospital when he was young. He tripped over some logs and broke his hip. He was in skeletal traction where a pin was placed in his leg, and he maintained bedrest for 6 weeks in the hospital, in a 12 bed ward, to help the fracture heal. He then went home, walking with crutches. He remembers going through the third or fourth grade on crutches when he was 8 or 9 years old. He recovered completely with a scar but no long term issues. The family had been familiar with Shriners Hospital before John's accident. James, the oldest son, stayed in and out of Shriners Hospital for extended periods up until age of 16, the age limit for Shriners at the time, having lost an arm and a leg, due to a bone development problem and possibly bone cancer. He endured much pain and was sick most of his life. Limb amputations and fitting for prosthetics required extended periods of hospitalizations at Shriners Hospital. He wore artificial limbs over a period of time. His leg prosthesis was state of the art for the mid-1940's. It was operated by means of pulleys and wires. James could bend his knee by moving his shoulder. James was fitted and cared for by "Mr. William Dewey Friddle, Sr., the first director of orthotics and prosthetics at Shriners in Greenville. His son would follow in his footsteps as the next director. The Friddle family is four generations strong in the profession."[49] I am proud to say I have personally known the last two generations for many years.

John recalled that with the leg prosthesis, James was required to wear a special shoe that the brace could fit in. They were able to obtain the shoe from a store on Main Street in Greenville. While regular shoes cost around a couple of dollars or so at the time, the special shoe James needed cost around $100. Even with all of the expert care that James would receive in and out of the hospital, he died at the age of 17 in the family home after much pain and suffering. Doris does not remember James as she was around 2 years old when he died. She was told of her daily interactions with James during his extended illness. She was told that she would enter James' room and go up to the bed. She would tell him that she was his baby sister, Doris, and ask him if he had anything for her. He would tell her hello and give her a piece of gum as he always kept gum at the bedside. He would hand her a piece and then she would go on her way. Even with no memory of him, she is left with a precious story.

Almost thirteen years after the death of James, their sixth born child Paul, would lose his life. Paul grew up with a problem with one of his legs. He wore a brace and used crutches and was a patient at Shriners Hospital in Greenville for several months at a time, just like his brother James. A diagnosis of their exact disease is not known among the family. James and Paul both had ailments where they were very frail, had a ruddy skin complexion, experienced lots of bone pain and joint discomfort. Both lost limbs from their condition and wore braces and walked with crutches or used a wheelchair at times. Tumors would develop in their bodies prior to their deaths, leading the siblings to believe their disease process was cancer related. Paul's story would differ some. While throwing a baseball with a friend, he got hit in the elbow. He then fell back and landed on the elbow and fractured his arm. After treatment with a cast for an extended time, a tumor was discovered when the cast was removed. His arm was amputated, and for a while things seemed to be okay. However, within a short period of time, he began to develop additional tumors throughout his body. His condition worsened so much that he required care by his family around the clock. During the last months his illness was so bad that he had two different physicians making house calls at different intervals to prescribe pain medication. Illness would claim his life at the age of twenty-five.

In their youth, the ailments didn't slow them down. James was an outdoors type and loved to hunt and camp. Months before Paul died, he worked in the store. He could do most anything with one arm, even sweep. The boys stated, "If you didn't work hard, he could make you look bad." Paul was known for his humor. After his hospital stay from his arm injury, his parents received a hospital bill. They looked over the charges and there was a one dollar charge for the Emergency Room. Someone asked Paul if he had gone to the emergency room before being admitted. He said he recalled walking in a hallway, and a door to the emergency room opened. Paul said he looked inside and saw a beautiful nurse standing at the nurse's station. He laughed and said they must have charged him for looking through the door. Paul was also known for his clothes. He was always dressed nice and had nice clothes to wear. Paul worked and saved his money for nice clothes. Doris and a brother stayed with him pretty much around the clock to help care for him. One of the last memories that Doris has of their interactions were centered on clothes. He gave Doris money and asked her to go to the department store in town and buy him a new pair of pants and a wind breaker type jacket. She brought them back and hung them on a hanger in his room in his view. He kept focusing on his new clothes and his ability one day to wear them. Doris said he never got to wear them. The morning of his death, several family members and some family friends were gathered at the bedside. Paul opened his eyes and asked who was sitting at the foot of his bed. When they replied no one, he replied "there are two people sitting there." Grandpa wondered if that was James and Lois waiting for him.

In between the deaths of James and Paul, the eldest daughter, Lois, had problems right after the birth of her second child, Reba. It is thought that she had issues with breast cancer prior to this. After giving birth, she hemorrhaged for multiple days and medical tests resulted in the diagnosis of leukemia. She was taken to her parents' home for constant care of her and the baby. Lois died in the family home less than three weeks after giving birth at the age of 30. Doris recalls that right before Lois died, the family was gathered around her bed. Grandpa would go to her every few minutes and ask her how she was doing and if she needed anything. On the final time he questioned her, she said she was getting a little dizzy. When asked if he could do anything she said she wanted to sing a song. As the family tried to start a song, they couldn't. Everyone was trying to hold back tears. At that time, Lois started to sing with her beautiful voice an old gospel hymn that contained the words "I feel like traveling on." She died shortly after that. Granny and Grandpa adopted her two children, Edna and Reba, and raised them. In a span of 13 years, death claimed three of the Head children, but the family was able to persevere. They continued to manage their businesses, raise children and grandchildren and still maintain a strong faith in God.

Grandpa held everyone together. Granny was very stoic. She didn't talk much about the deaths of her children or show many emotions, but everyone knew she held them close to her heart.

It amazes me how the family managed to hold the businesses together, stay close to each other and help support each other. In the younger years, trips to visit the kids while hospitalized could be very challenging. A trip to Shriners in Greenville and back in itself took almost a day. Visiting hours would be limited as well. Upon occasion, I believe that some of the hospitalization stays overlapped, and they had two children hospitalized at the same time. The stress of having sick children, running multiple businesses and maintaining a large household for Grandpa and Granny must have been quite challenging at times. Once the kids would return home from a hospital stay, the siblings would pitch in to care for them. It was hard to see them in pain and sick, but they were a family unit. They were loyal to the end with a strong faith to get through those tough times.

When Paul became ill over his last months, the married children came by to visit. Doris recalls that both Lola and Harold worked evening shift at the mill and would come over after work to visit with him. My mom and dad visited as well. My brother David recalls my dad telling him about his visits with Paul. My dad was not saved at the time and Paul would always talk to him about receiving Christ as his Savior. My dad told David that on his last visit with Paul, Paul talked to him and told my dad he was praying for him. It really touched my dad and David believes that lead to my dad's salvation.

Chapter Fourteen

STORIES INVOLVING THE UNKNOWN

THERE ARE LOTS of tales of ghost stories in the state of South Carolina, so it goes to think that the Head family would have a few to recall. It is suspected from several of the siblings that their family members all dying in the house left some unresolved issues. All three of the children were cared for during their illness and died in that same front bedroom. Various family members, especially Doris, spent many hours caring for Paul's needs. A short time before his death, Paul told family members and his minister that he saw a man sitting on the foot of his bed keeping him company. No one else could see this man.

Doris had spent much of her early teen years helping care for Paul. Sometime after he had died, she decided to move into the front bedroom. Unusual things began to occur in that room. One of the granddaughters was going to sleep in that room with Doris one night. Suddenly, she started crying and refused to stay there. She went back to her Granny. Doris stood on a chair to reach the light on/off pull cord. Although no one was in the room with her, something popped her on the head. She did not remember anything until she awoke in the bed the next morning. She heard the sound of feet shuffling across the floor and paper rattling. One night a cold hand grabbed Doris in the small of her back, and she couldn't move or scream. On several occasions she would hear breathing in the room. When Doris would tell her mom about these occurrences, she would be told not to talk about such things, that her Pa wouldn't like it. People would say they were crazy. However, strange things continued. A locked musical stationary box that had belonged to Paul was kept on the chest of drawers between the front door and window. During the night Doris was awakened to the tune "Oh! Susanna" playing from the locked music box. When Paul was alive and had the box, the tune played only when it was opened. Now it played when the box was closed and locked. Doris told her parents, siblings, and her best friend, Betty. To show Doris that she was just dreaming or imagining these things, her brother John spent the night in the bedroom. He also reported hearing footsteps, shuffling, and crackling of paper during the night. He, too, felt the grip of a cold hand that grabbed him in the back and prevented him from moving or speaking. Mose also slept in the room out of curiosity. The next morning he said, "Something grabbed me. I tried to call for help, but no one came! Why didn't ya'll come?" No one had heard him. When these events first began to occur, they mainly happened when the room was occupied by one person and only during the night. That changed. They began happening during the day and in other rooms of the house. Again, Grandpa didn't want these things to be told because of what other people might say. Because she could not get a good night's sleep at home, Doris began spending the night with her friend Betty, or Betty would stay the night with her. She and Betty would often sleep in the room next to Grandpa and Granny instead of the front bedroom. Betty had been told by her mother that if you see a strange phenomenon, you should ask it, "What in the name of the Lord do you want?" When Doris and Betty saw a blue laser-like light moving around the room, Betty did just that. The light quickly moved across the guitar that previously had belonged to Doris's deceased brother James. A loud, discordant strum of guitar strings sounded as the light streaked across it. Doris told Lola what was going on, and Lola told her mom that she needed to listen to Doris and check into things.

In spite of their original protestations that nothing was going on, Granny and Grandpa also experienced some unexplained things. On one occasion, he heard the toenails of a dog walking across the wooden floors. The sound went to each door of the bedroom, but stopped and did not enter. "You forgot to put the dog out," he told Granny. Her response was, "We don't have a dog" and they did not have a dog at that time. A search of the house did not find a stray! They also heard the sound of random bangs on the piano in the living room when no one else was present. On one occasion Granny heard someone walking in the front room and followed the sound through the house and into the kitchen where she saw the screen door open and then slam closed. Another day she was combing her hair in her bedroom when she heard breathing coming from the wardrobe. She opened the door and saw something dark with its arms and legs folded up in there. It leaped out, unfolding itself. Being fearless, Granny grabbed her broom and chased the thing while yelling, "Get out of this house!"

A lady minister was preaching during an evening service at their church. Because of the late hour at which the service ended, it was decided that she would stay the night in their home. As one might expect, they put her in the front bedroom which was now the guest room. She definitely experienced some distress during the night and told them the next morning, "There is something wrong in that bedroom." Grandpa finally agreed that something had to be done. He talked to a reverend from Alabama, who was preaching a revival in Central. He told the reverend what was going on and asked him to come to the house. In preparation for that visit, they were asked to remove all old medicines and equipment and such that had been used with their deceased children from the house. When he came, they walked through each room of the house, read Bible verses, and prayed and asked for blessings on this home. There were no more reports of strange happenings. A nearby neighbor later told Grandpa and Granny that at the time that visit was taking place, she was sitting on her front porch and saw a blue light lift from the top of their house and move up into the air. She had not known about the prayers that were going on in their house at that time. After the front bedroom was cleaned and redecorated, there were no further reports of anything strange in that bedroom. Later on, the room became a storage room and remained so for many years. These events lead to the naming of the character in question, Sir Simon. It was given this name later on by some of the grandchildren from a TV character of long ago, as they heard the stories.

Several years after the deaths of Grandpa and Granny, the house mysteriously burned. John, the fire chief, and the other firemen responded quickly but the house was fully engulfed. When it was determined that the house was about to collapse, the firemen pulled back. Although the streets to that area were blocked, an old car sped up to the house, a man jumped out and insisted there was someone in the house, and that he and John could save him. John told the man that the house was empty and about to fall in. The stranger insisted that he had been at fires before and knew how to save the man. A silhouette of a man wearing a hat and standing at a front window was pointed out by the stranger. John saw what appeared to be a man just standing at the front window. John said the silhouette looked like his dad wearing one of his hats that he always wore. The insistent man kept urging John to get closer to the house. John noticed the man's hands looked brown and burned. The wall fell, missing John by mere inches. The strange man left as quickly as he had arrived. No one knew him or ever saw him again. John stated that he thinks that man was the devil and was trying to get him close enough so the wall would fall on him. Sometimes real life can't be explained easily.

Chapter Fifteen

PASSING OF A GENERATION

GRANNY DIED ON December 26, 1985, during the night after Christmas day. She got sick and some of the kids were called, who in turn called an ambulance. As they were getting her on the gurney to get her in the ambulance, she stopped them and told them she needed her hat. Granny always wore a hat, summer or winter that she had crocheted. They got her hat and put it on her head and off she went. She died soon after getting in the ambulance. Doris recalls seeing a bank sign that told time and temperature as they followed the ambulance to the hospital. It showed 2 degrees that night. She needed her hat indeed. Granny had a history of heart failure and that is believed to be the cause of her death.

Grandpa lived for almost 2 years longer. He developed diabetes and died in Easley Hospital on November 2, 1987. At his bedside were several family members, when he passed. His heart had stopped and his EKG had flat lined (showed no rhythm or heart beat). As this occurred, Pastor Bob and his wife Clara were at the bedside and sang to him and talked to him about crossing over the Jordan. Grandpa raised his head up in the bed and tried to speak before lying back down. The family knew he was making his way home. He had fought a good fight and finished his race.

Years later Ernest would die in 1993. Annie died in 2013 and Lola died in 2015. The three remaining siblings survive today even though they have battled illnesses as well.

Both Granny and Grandpa's final physical landmarks lie in Mt Zion Cemetery in Central along with several of their children gone on. On all of their tombstones are their names and the birth date and date of death listed. Those dates signify a beginning and an end. The time between those dates for each of their lives represents so many memories and tales that I have attempted to tell in this book.

Grandpa and Granny

Chapter Sixteen

MOVING FORWARD

REFLECTING UPON THE stories told and the ones I have
fondly recalled, I sit amazed. I ask the same question I posed in the
opening of this book; how did I get here? I am now able to visualize
a masterpiece painting. All of the brushstrokes that I see represent
different sizes of brushes, various colors and types of paint that all
came together. Each stroke is filled with memories and stories. All
represent roads taken, decisions made and characters developed.
These brushstrokes represent a hard work ethic, simplicity, pain and
sorrow, beauty, humor, intelligence, creativity, strength and many
other characteristics, each one leading to my path. The masterpiece
may show a landscape of trees and waterfalls and streams or a piece
of farmland with tractors, hay and cattle. It may represent a portrait
of a couple or one of a family. A church, store or buildings may be in
the background. The masterpiece is unique, dynamic and priceless.
What comes to mind for me as I reflect upon the past is the scripture
of Jeremiah 1:5. "Before I formed thee in the belly I knew thee; and
before thou camest forth out of the womb I sanctified thee, and I
ordained thee a prophet unto the nations."

I look back at the stories and ask what if World War I had not
ended when it did, and my grandfather did go overseas to fight in
the war? He may never have made it back. What if the man on the
train had not unlocked the door, and thus Grandpa was unable
to get inside the train? He may have died. What if Granny said
no rather than yes to attending a dance with Grandpa back in the

1920s? They may have never married nor had children. If any one of these, what appear to be isolated events, did not happen the way they did, it could have changed the course of life as I know it today. If my grandparents never got together, I would not be here. My Uncle John often wondered why a brother older than him and one younger than him, and he being the son in the middle of those two in age, never suffered the same illness as they did. Why did he live until the age of 57 before becoming ill with cancer that was treated? Even though I never heard my mom mention it, she probably asked the same question as she was a middle child between James and Paul as well, and never suffered any illness. I am totally amazed and overwhelmed when I look back at things that either did or did not happen according to God's plan. My grandparents never flew in an airplane or saw a laptop computer or cell phone, but they did see the good in people, the effects of hard work, and the benefits of a strong faith. As I continue to move forward, I still recall the characters of these tales and their zest and energy for life and serving others. Characteristics, genetics and names have more meaning than ever before. Establishing and polishing landmarks are important.

All of the information and stories have been shared in the most accurate way to the best of the knowledge of my siblings, cousins, aunt and uncles. The integrity of the stories from the children passed down to their children to the memories from the three remaining Head children has been recorded and maintained to the best of our ability. As you read the stories, it is hoped the information generated memories of many wonderful people today and those who have already passed on. One may see where a name originated or see qualities of themselves in some of the actions. As the information is shared, it is hoped that the courage, strength, intelligence, love and faith demonstrated and shared in these stories will live on and be further demonstrated on a daily basis by the life we live and pass on to others.

After reading this, I ask you to self-reflect. What does God have left for you to do? Are there things you can do to improve your journey and final destination? Have you accepted Jesus Christ as your Lord and Savior? If not, I plead with you to do so today. Seek His presence and His salvation. Next, are there relationships within your family that are broken and in need of repair? If so, take the first step to mend it. Maybe you have tried. Try again. Do you have friendships that have been severed or have been left with unresolved issues? Ask God to help you. If relationships aren't broken, but you haven't seen someone in a long time, make an effort to change that. Call someone or text someone to say "Hello, I am thinking about you." Try to visit family and friends when you can and as often as you can. Ask family about their past if they are still living. What was their childhood like? Learning about others, especially your family can help you to learn more about yourself. Ask yourself if you are leaving anything behind for others? Are you leaving landmarks? Did you make a difference in someone's day or their life in general? We often spend most of our life moving forward, or at least are trying to do so. We make plans to move forward and direct our future. As I have gotten older, however, I have learned that it is often when we look backward, we can learn the most. My grandparents made a difference. My parents made a difference. Did I? When my journey ends, the scripture I want to resonate is 2 Timothy 4:7. I have fought a good fight. I have finished my course, I have kept the faith. May each of us become a part of the plan that God has for us and we be obedient to his calling. May we develop new landmarks worthy of others searching for them.

Lois Edna

Lola Francis

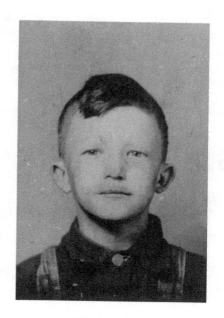

James Arthur

Annie Laura

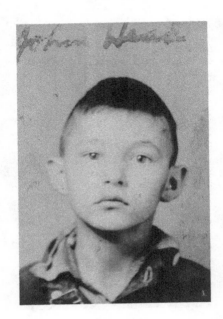

Johnny Ray

Paul Edward

Charles Elzie

Ernest Franklin

Doris Louise

Seated from left to right: Annie, Doris Standing from left to right: Ernest, Charles, John, Lola

Granny and Grandpa around their 62nd Anniversary

SUMMARY

A small Southern town in the Upstate of South Carolina, known as Central, is the main setting for the Head family and the many stories shared and passed down for generations. These stories are intertwined with legends, tales, and historical facts to examine life in the early to mid-1900's. Other locations in South Carolina and Western North Carolina are included in these stories as well.

Life at a simple place and time, long before technology ruled the world, is presented. Even though simple and basic, this way of life served as the foundation for growth and the opportunities seen today. Armed with ingenuity, intelligence, and a strong work ethic, numerous business endeavors were developed. Having limitless faith, as well as the ability to love and to see the good in people, the Head family forged generations of good will. The love of God and Country was practiced. Landmarks were developed and remain in place today for others to follow.

AUTHOR BIO

ANN ROWLAND HAMLIN is a native of Central, South Carolina. She graduated from DW Daniel High School in Central. She attended Clemson University and received a Bachelor of Science in nursing and later obtained a Master of Science in nursing as well. After a nursing career spanning almost thirty years, she is retired. She loves to cook, travel and cheer for her Clemson Tigers. She is a cat mom to five fur babies. Faith and family are her passions. This book was written as a work of love to share with her family and future generations.

ENDNOTES

1   Rickie Longfellow. Wagons West. United states Department of Transportation: Federal Highway Administration. Last updated 6/27/2017 https://fhwa.dot.gov/infrastructure/back0307.cfm

2   Ford Motor Company Timeline. https://corporate.ford.com / history.html (access Date March 24, 2020).

3   Wilt Browning, Marlene Burke and Doris Browning. *Come Quittin' Time: From Child Laborer to Family Matriarch, a Mother's Lifetime Spent in Southern Cotton Mills.* (Kernersville, NC: Alabaster, 2007) 5

4   Marcy Thompson "Picturing the Past: Rosman Had Several Previous Names." *The Transylvania Times.* July 21, 2014 https://www.transylvaiatimes.com/story/2014/07/21/lifestyles/rosman

5   Marcy Thompson . "Picturing the Past: Hayes, Silversteen Developed Upper End of County." *The Transylvania Times.* July 28, 2014 https://www.transylvaiatimes.com/story/2014/07/28/lifestles/hayes

6   Leigh Ann Henion. "The Beauty of the French Broad River: Follow an ancient river through Appalachia to explore one of the South's most stunning landscapes." *Southern Living.* https://www.southernliving.com/travel/north-carolina/french-broad-river (access Date July 2, 2019)

7   "Transylvania Always." Transylvania County Tourism Development Authority. 2017. https://explorebrevard.com/the-great-outdoors/forests-parks/rs

8   Hurley E. Badders, Oconee County. *South Carolina Encyclopedia* http://www.scencyclopedia.org/sce/entries/oconee-county/ (access Date March 25, 2020)

9   Joseph Gauzens, *Salem, Twice a Town* (Salem, S.C. : 1993) 1

10 Badders, Oconee County. (access Date March 25, 2020)

11 Duke Energy. Our History. https://www.duke-energy.com/our-company/about-us/our-history (access Date March 25, 2020)

12 Badders, Oconee County. (access Date March 24, 2020)

13 E Don Herd, Jr. *The South Carolina Upcountry, 1540-1980: Historical and Biographical Sketches.* Volume1. (Greenwood, SC: The Attic Press, 1981) 85-91

14 Robert M. Dunkerly and Eric K. Williams. *Old Ninety-Six: A History and Guide* (Charleston: History Press,2006), 11-12.

15 *Descendants of Frederick Whitmire.* Ancestry.com http:/ancestrylibrary.com/search/?name=frederick_whitmire&birth=1742 (access Date on August 1, 2019)

16 Bert Sitton. Descendents of William Gillespie. Ancestry.com http:/ancestrylibrary.com/search/?namewilliam_gillespie&birth=1720 (access Date on August 1, 2019)

17 Descendents of William Gillespie. Ancestry.comhttp:/ancestrylibrary.com/search/?namewilliam_gillespie&birth=1720 (access Date on August 1, 2019)

18 Paul E Rice. *Descendants of Stephen Rice*. Ancestry.com http:/ ancestrylibrary.com/search/?name=stephen_rice&birth=1637 (access Date on August 2, 2019)

19 Descendants of Alston Head. Ancestry.com http://ancestrylibrary.com/search/?name=alston-head&birth=1807 (accesse Date on August 2 ,2019)

20 Michael Hembree and Dot Jackson. *Keowee. The Story of the Keowee River Valley in the Upstate South Carolina.* (South Carolina: 1997). 71,74

21 Wilt Browning, Marlene Burke and Doris Browning, 58

22 Debbie Fletcher. *Whipporwill Farewell: Jocassee Remembered* (North America: Trafford Publishing, 2003) 39

23 Piper Peters Aheron. *Images of America: Pickens County* (Charleston, SC: Arcadia Publishing, 2008) 6-8

24 Mattie May Morgan Allen. *Central Yesterday and Today* (Faith Printing Company: Taylors, South Carolina, 1973) 26-27

25 Aheron, *Images*, 38

26 Allen, *Central Yesterday and Today*, 42

27 Jerry Alexander. *Living, Loving and Dying From Payday to Payday In A Southern Cotton Mill Village.The Cateechee Story* 4th ed. (Seneca, SC: 2009) 7-9

28 Aheron, Images 38

29 Ben Robertson and Lacy K. Ford. *Red Hills and Cotton: an upcountry memory* (University of South Carolina Press, 1991) 274-277

30 Brantli Jane Owens. *Images of America: Easley* (Charleston, SC: Arcadia Publishing, 2008) 39.

31 Browning, Burke and Browning. 156

32 *Noelle Talmon, contributor for Ripleys.com* https://www.ripleys. com/weird-news/funeral-homes-ambulances/ (access Date on July 2, 2019)

33 Jerry Alexander, *The Cateechee Story: A Little Place called Cateechee.* 3rd ed. (Seneca, SC: 2004) 39-41

34 Wikipedia contributors, "South Carolina Highway 93," *Wikipedia, The Free Encyclopedia,* https://en.wikipedia.org/w/index. php?title=South_Carolina_Highway_93&oldid=822562600 (access Date on April 8, 2020).

35 Wallace R. Griffitts and Jerry C. Olson. *Mica Deposits of the Southeastern Piedmont: Part 7. Hartwell District, Georgia and South Carolina. Part 8. Outlying Deposits in South Carolina Geological Survey Professional Paper 248-E* US GPO, Washington: 1953 . https://pubs.usgs.gov/pp/0248e/report. pdf (access Date on July 2, 2019)

36 Griffits and Olson, 1953

37 Paul Clark. *Digging deep into Western North Carolina's mining history.* Smoky Mountain Living Magazine. June 1, 2013, https://www.smliv.com/stories/ digging-deep-into-western-north-carolinas-mining-history/

38 Ben Robertson and Lacy K. Ford. *Red Hills and Cotton: an upcountry memory* (University of South Carolina Press, 1991) 122

39 Susan Lefler . *Images of America: Brevard. (Charleston, SC: Arcadia Publishing,* 2004) 123

40 Dennis Glazener. *Gunmakers of North Carolina.* Descendents of William Gillespie. Ancestry.com http:/ancestrylibrary.com/

search/?namewilliam_gillespie&birth=1720 (access Date on August 1, 2019)

41 Lynn Warren, "Gun-maker carries on tradition of his ancestors" *Chesterfield Observer* 2007 https://www.chesterfieldobserver. com/articles/gun-maker-carries-on-tradition-of-his-ancestors

42 Bert Sitton. Descendents of William Gillespie. Ancestry. com http:/ancestrylibrary.com/search/?namewilliam_gilles-pie&birth=1720 (accessed on 8/1/19)

43 History of Clemson Blue Cheese. Clemson University https:// www.clemson.edu/bluecheese/history.html (access Date March 23,2020)

44 Robert Tate. The early years of Ford tractors (1907-1961). Motorcities. org Posted 3/27/2017 https://www.motorcitie s .or g / s tor y- o f - the-week/2017

45 Kirk H. Neely. *A Good Mule is Hard to Find.* (Hub City Press: 2009) 100 Neely, 110

46 Neely, 110

47 Rebecca Lang. "8 things only southerners know about tea." *Food Network.* https://foodnetwork.com (access Date on April 8, 2020)

48 History. Shriners Hospital for Children–Greenville. https:// www.shrinershospitalsforchildren.org/greenville/about-us

49 Frank Friddle, personal interview. September 11, 2020.

CPSIA information can be obtained
at www.ICGtesting.com
Printed in the USA
BVHW080136240221
600893BV00008B/679